The
Delivery Room

Discovering the real me in Him…

By

Kika Ashanike

"***Low self-esteem***, rejection***, jealousy*** and backbiting, ***losing a first love***, break ups and ***make ups*** and serving ***God*** in a God less world…"

For <u>*every*</u> young woman in Christ x

The
Delivery Room

Copyright © 2013 Kika Ashanike

www.kikseeks.com

For special discounts regarding bulk purchases or to book the author for a speaking engagement please email bookingsforkiks@hotmail.co.uk

The author takes speaking engagements for the following; TV, radio, churches, conferences, universities, schools and business engagements to inspire women or young people.

ISBN 978-1490924793

TABLE OF CONTENTS

Introduction

Chapter 1   Will you be made whole?

Chapter 2   Will you be obedient?

Chapter 3   The stink of rejection

Chapter 4   Battling loneliness

Chapter 5   Don't give away God's affection

Chapter 6   Death by paper cuts

Chapter 7   Knowing the Lord's voice

Chapter 8   Unhealthy ties

Chapter 9   Dry your eyes

Chapter 10   Living for more than me

Chapter 11   Don't rush the process

Chapter 12   A new way of living

ACKNOWLEDGEMENTS

My wonderful family and friends, thank you guys for your support and for believing in me. I literally have the best family and friends anyone could ever ask for.

Love you guys x

DEDICATION

To all those seeking joy, peace and a true and intimate relationship with God; I hope that the words that He has given me are able to help you to discover your true identity in Christ which will allow you to receive all of these things.

Feel free to enter into this delivery room where God can guide you and I through all of the things stopping us from having an intimate relationship with Him and into a life of true joy and freedom.

The Delivery Room

INTRODUCTION

Knowing how to start this is definitely a huge blur but here goes everything. I'm Kika and I run a women's ministry called Pure Hearts. I gave my life to Christ at the age of 17 and I'm 23 now, 6 years in and it's definitely been an interesting ride. I started my journey with Christ by going to a weekly youth gathering based in London, then it was a church, then out of church and kind of sort of church again. But in all of the ins and outs of places I was able to find and develop a personal relationship with God for myself, a relationship that went beyond a youth gathering, church walls and anything else in between. Although so much was learnt along the way the one thing that remains close to my heart is the strong dislike of seeing people (especially females) going through heartache and pain, low self-esteem and or lack of self-worth. I guess you could say deep calls unto deep?

I have been able to develop a relationship with God where He has become real, true and a permanent and a so very much cherished fixture in my life. He has become Abba, comforter, healer, redeemer, best friend and everything else I couldn't even have ever imagined. He speaks, He cares and He is forever by me and always for me. He has shown me a love that

I never thought existed, given me a hope in a future that I didn't truly believe in and filled me with a joy and peace that surpasses all understanding.

My heart and my passion are to help other people to know and understand that this same God can become real in their lives too. He loves and cares for you like He does anyone else. The only problem is that there are so many things in the way of us being able to receive that love. Some of those things include, but are not limited to; low self-esteem, a lack of self-love, heartbreak following the breakdown of a relationship, a sense of hopelessness, not understanding the reason for one's existence or simply feeling unloved.

The truth is that being a young Christian woman can be so lonely. On any given Sunday we can attend church and hear the pastor speak on how God can lift us out of dark places and bad seasons in our lives. He or she then goes on to give examples of these dark places in life which often includes examples such as; losing a child, not having enough money to pay the rent and wondering where your next meal will come from, being stuck in the same place for 40 years like the children of Israel, going through a divorce and much more similar instances. This message is great and it sure does touch the hearts of almost 80 percent of the congregation, but what about us? What about those of us whose dark place and bad season isn't in a divorce, or struggling to pay rent, or being stuck in the same place for years? What if our dark place is in losing a boyfriend, not feeling as pretty as a best friend, wondering if we'll ever get married and if anyone will ever want us, having a bad childhood experience, feeling unloved, fear for our future, not feeling comfortable in our own skin, wishing we were different, feeling rejected, on the verge of depression, battling temptation, loneliness, wondering if I'm in the "right religion" or wanting to live a non-Christian lifestyle? Does this mean that God doesn't care about our dark place or that our pain isn't justified? ... No my sweetheart, It doesn't. It means emphasis isn't placed on it but it doesn't take away the fact that God loves us and wants us free to be able to serve Him and enjoy our lives. There is no common problem amongst us all, but there sure is one common solution, I have found God to be that solution.

This book is one that addresses the pain of this group of young women. It aims to help young Christian women struggling with anything from low self-esteem to heartbreak to be able to enter into a delivery room, where together we can work on getting rid of all these negatives and begin to create a clear path, to allow God's love that has been hindered for too long to be able to freely flow into our lives and into our hearts. I can promise you He brings only good things, He gets rid of fear, heartache, pain, shame, low self-esteem, lack and bondage and replaces it with love, hope, peace, joy, faith, a sound mind, strength, boldness and courage. He truly does help you to deliver a brand new you; a you that looks exactly like His son Jesus Christ. If you are willing, please read on and stay with me on this journey in the delivery room.

> *It won't be easy (I hear giving birth never is) but I've also heard it's so worth it! You can do this....*

I will start by speaking a little on willingness and obedience, as although we are willing, we must also be obedient to His every word should we truly wish to give birth to a new us!

The Delivery Room

CHAPTER 1

WILL YOU BE MADE WHOLE?

No doubt you have picked up this book because you have dealt with or are dealing with some form of emotional pain. I have no doubt that you want to be free of that pain and wish to live a life of peace and of internal joy. This is a very good decision that you have made. Many people feel emotional pain and go through hard times, however a shocking fact is that half of the pain that most of us are feeling we actually have the power to put a stop to. If many more of us would step out and make the choice to make some changes and or remove ourselves from certain situations or lifestyles, peace and joy would be the end result of our everyday lives. If you are in a relationship that is causing you immense heartache, have such low self-esteem that you are crippled with fear and self-doubt, constantly complain about hating your life or you feel like you are not as close to God or know him the way that you want to know him, then my question to you is, what are you doing to change this?

I pose the above question because many of us are in a position where we are hurting and constantly we pray to God that He change our situations and "make things better", but I've been forced to learn that God works *with us* to make visible changes in our lives. Sometimes we must approach the spiritual with the same application that we use for the physical. If you didn't like feeling the cold during the times of winter you wouldn't just hope and pray for warmth, you would buy a coat to shield you from the cold, take vitamins to boost your immune system and wear layers of clothing to protect your body from feeling the now bitter and rainy weather. So once again, if something is causing you pain or a lack of fullness of joy, what are *you* doing to change it?

The decision to make a change and the application of this decision by deliberate actions taken is what is required for God to begin a work in you and make visible changes in your life. You must make the conscious decision to get well! Are *you willing* to be made whole? Because until you are, there truly is little sense to the tears that you cry or the prayers that you are praying for change, you must first and foremost be willing to be made whole. In the book of John chapter 5 (KJV), Jesus asked a man that had lay sick for 38 years "wilt though be made whole?" On the face of it that question would appear a rather absurd question, of course a man that has been left immobile for 38 years desires badly to be made whole? But clearly not, because if the One who knows all things posed the question to him, it is clear the question had to be asked. I believe Jesus posed this question because the first point to be dealt with when a person is in a bad state, is whether or not that person is truly ready to live life in a new way and get away from the "illness" that they are in. You would be surprised how many of us (including at one time you and me) have made constant excuses as to why we couldn't yet "get well" or how hard we found it to live God's way, what is even more shocking is how many of us simply enjoy rolling round in the mess that we are in. But I thank God that now we are at a place where we are ready to put aside excuses and have become willing to be made whole. You making the decision to pick up this book is a sure sign to me that you are willing to move forward into better.

However, our willingness must be demonstrated through obedience. When we say that we are willing to be made whole or willing to completely live life God's way then we must be obedient to His every word as He guides us out of "situations" into complete wholeness.

Before we dive into the intricate parts of this book I warn you sis, healing is a process, it is not something that can be rushed or hurried through. Be willing to walk the long walk to your own freedom, be willing to obey His voice as He guides you through, and lastly enjoy the process. Enjoy the process of God helping you to get free from the past and move into a great future. It may take tears, times of feeling low from the issues that arise that you have to deal with, dealing with issues of the past that you may have thought of as unimportant or left buried deep within, but I guarantee you, if God started the healing process in you He will complete it. Your only job is to obey and rest in Him and He will carry you through. We will now go on to discuss this key word obedience. What is it and why is it so important? Please stay with me as we read together.

I'm rooting for you Sis and so is he...You can do this...

The Delivery Room

CHAPTER 2

WILL YOU BE OBEDIENT?

It took me a while to piece together the puzzle of my purpose. I'm what you would call an eclectic person so I enjoy doing lots of different things. One day I wanted to be a lawyer, another I wanted to be business woman, I wanted to write, I wanted to teach, I wanted to do this and that. I often wondered how I would piece it all together, or maybe I had to pray to see which one God was saying I had to do or He wanted me to do. I went to university and studied law; I started a charity which allowed me to do what you would call ministry; I started a company which would allow me to do business. But yet was I fulfilling my purpose? Was I even on the way to fulfilling my purpose? No. It wasn't until recently that I realised that my purpose and calling was the same as yours and the same as Christ's, my purpose is obedience.

We spend so long wondering what our purpose is, "why was I created", "for what great purpose am I here" that we completely miss the true reason we were born. We were born to have a relationship with the Father, an intimate relationship that sees us be obedient to his every word. I believe that we all have the exact same purpose, to become one with God here on earth, to be able to have a relationship with him where He speaks to us and we talk back to Him. When we truly understand this we come to the realisation that the scriptures are true when they state that God is no respecter of persons.[1] I often wondered why some peoples "purpose" may have been to be great high flying business persons with a ton of wealth whilst others was to act as a church usher. No disrespect to church ushers they do a great job but come on, that's a vast difference between the two. But when I understood that we all have the same purpose, to serve God and to be obedient to His every word I began to see God truly is no respecter of persons. He may give us different pathways to fulfil this obedience unto Him but it is all for the same purpose-whether a millionaire or someone on state benefits our purpose is to be obedient to the Father, giving and bringing unto Him all the glory which He truly deserves. It was amazing when I realised this because it also helped me to break a habit of jealousy. When we realise that we all have the same purpose we need not be jealous or envious of what someone else is doing, their purpose is exactly the same as mine, they just have a different way which God has given them to fulfil that purpose.

---

[1] Acts 10:34 KJV

With that said I would like to speak a little more on obedience as before you can even enter the delivery room to begin dealing with issues of the heart, you must first master obedience. You do this by simply making up your mind to be obedient. God wants to heal you and set you free of whatever it may be that you are struggling with, but will you listen? Will you obey?

> *I know it's not so easy to obey Sis, but it truly is what is best for us…You can do this…*

I heard a pastor say recently that "your purpose and your destiny is locked up in your obedience". I think that line may just have gone someway to changing and taking my obedience level up a gear. I always believed the word destiny meant something that was inevitable. I've often heard people say "if you're meant to have it you will", "if it's your destiny it will happen", "no one can stop your destiny". Lies! For starters the devil can stop your destiny and oh how he very much tries. We hear stories of little children raped at the age of 2, some even as young as a few days old and we think "oh how wicked the devil is". But more importantly we have to think of why the enemy is so intent on destroying people from such a young age. I believe it is to mess them up from so young that they have no choice but to miss what God had prepared for them in their future. I also believe that the devil has a helper who helps him in allowing us to miss our destiny. That helper is us! So many times we give the devil a hand and help him along in his quest to make us miss our destiny. Some of us do such a good job that he doesn't even need to do very much, he's able to put his feet up, watch some TV and we even make him a coffee and fluff his pillows to make sure he's nice and comfortable. But the enemy is only able to do this when we are disobedient to God. When we get ourselves aligned with God and what His will is daily for our lives and we obey as He leads then we are able to remain in His perfect will and there and only there are we safe and protected, our heart kept safe and protected and so is the task which God has set us to do on the earth. This is particularly important in the area of emotional healing as the phrase "time is a greater healer" will not help set us free because the truth is that God is the Healer and if we allow Him through obedience to His guidance in our time of need, we will be made whole. We will be set free if we abide in Him and remain obedient to Him. Psalm 91 says it perfectly when it says "He that dwelleth in the secret place of the most high shall abide under the shadow of the almighty" (KJV). Many people claim this scripture and that is not surprising. What an amazing thing it is to be able to dwell in the secret place of God. But the key word here is "dwell". The word "dwell" means to "live as a resident, to reside"[2]. When we live somewhere we do so because we decide to live there, we make the purposeful decision to be in this place and choose to make it our home because it was our favourite of all the other houses we looked at. We purposely *chose* to live there. This is the same when we choose to live and dwell (be obedient) in the secret place with God, it is a choice because our God never has and would never force us to do anything against our will! (Such a gentleman we serve).

However, unlike a physical house the secret place of God is not somewhere we can use and abuse. We cannot choose to walk in and out freely as we wish and stroll back home at 2 in the morning or whatever time pleases us. This is in fact a sacred place that we are never to leave. It is an invisible house that we sleep in, go to work in, go to class in, go to dinner in, put our makeup on or off in, the secret place of God is somewhere we are to permanently remain in. That is to say that when you have made the decision to be obedient to God in your journey with Him and through the process of Him healing your heart you need to make it a

---

[2] Psalm 91:1 KJV

priority to ensure that your obedience does not waver. Decide to stay in the secret place and remain there! Now I don't know about you but that is a place where I never want to leave and I pray nothing ever entices me strongly enough that I freely and stupidly and dangerously walk out of it. I pray if you are not yet there you are obedient enough to enter in and that if you are there you are obedient enough to remain. Let me share some of the wonderful reasons why we should remain in this place with you.

Psalm 91 (KJV)

[1]He that dwelleth in the secret place of the most High shall abide under the shadow of the Almighty.

[2]I will say of the LORD, He is my refuge and my fortress: my God; in him will I trust.

[3]Surely he shall deliver thee from the snare of the fowler, and from the noisome pestilence.

[4]He shall cover thee with his feathers, and under his wings shalt thou trust: his truth shall be thy shield and buckler.

[5]Thou shalt not be afraid for the terror by night; nor for the arrow that flieth by day;

⁶Nor for the pestilence that walketh in darkness; nor for the destruction that wasteth at noonday.

⁷A thousand shall fall at thy side, and ten thousand at thy right hand; but it shall not come nigh thee.

⁸Only with thine eyes shalt thou behold and see the reward of the wicked.

⁹Because thou hast made the LORD, which is my refuge, even the most High, thy habitation;

¹⁰There shall no evil befall thee, neither shall any plague come nigh thy dwelling.

¹¹For he shall give his angels charge over thee, to keep thee in all thy ways.

¹²They shall bear thee up in their hands, lest thou dash thy foot against a stone.

¹³Thou shalt tread upon the lion and adder: the young lion and the dragon shalt thou trample under feet.

¹⁴Because he hath set his love upon me, therefore will I deliver him: I will set him on high, because he hath known my name.

¹⁵He shall call upon me, and I will answer him: I will be with him in trouble; I will deliver him, and honour him.

¹⁶With long life will I satisfy him, and shew him my salvation.

Amen!

> *I pray that psalm blessed you Sis...you can do this...*

Disobedience will cause you to miss your destiny

I have often heard of and witnessed many people called out from a crowd and prophesied over. A preacher has told you that you will be this and you will be that, you will be used by God in this way and that way. That is great. But I have news for you, that doesn't mean that thing will happen. That is your destiny yes, but if you fail to fulfil your daily and primary purpose of obedience you will miss this very thing that was prophesied over you. Being called out of a crowd, God himself showing you a vision of what he will have you be, waking up to an angel at 3 o clock in the morning that tells you that you are chosen, all that great stuff will not even seal and stamp your destiny. Only your obedience will. Because your "purpose and your destiny is locked up in your obedience". Let's take a look at some scriptural examples.

God said to Adam in Genesis "be fruitful, multiply and replenish the earth".[3] Now notice, no preacher told Adam his purpose, no evangelist called him out of the crowd, God himself told Adam face to face, his purpose. You would think that was the ultimate seal to mean his destiny would come to pass. But no! Even though God said it, the application of it lay in Adams obedience. His disobedience to God (by the eating of a fruit from the forbidden tree) led to Adam missing his destiny. Should Adam have lived in his daily purpose of being obedient to God's every word he would have continued on to fulfil his purpose as God had ordained. Prophesised to you or not, disobedience will make you to miss your destiny.

Now it's important to notice that any disobedience can make you to miss your destiny. Adam's destiny was to subdue the earth and to be the ruler of the earth (literally), all he did was eat a fruit and yet he missed his destiny. Anyone would think such a "small sin" as we so wrongfully like to refer to such would not negate such a big destiny. But this is a clear example to us that no sin is small and no sin is

---

[3] Genesis 1:28 KJV

big, sin is sin. I mean the world is the way it is today because one man ate a fruit! Sin is sin people!

However, there is good news! As such as disobedience to God's instructions for us can cause us to miss our destiny or at times delay it, obedience to God's words for us and to us causes us to attain the things that God has prepared for us. The greatest example of this is the wonderful Jesus. His obedience unto death is such a great example for us of how to be constantly obedient to God even when it hurts, even when it is painful and sometimes even when we don't understand. I love the Jesus that we see in the garden of Gethsemane because for me it truly displayed his humanity.[4] We see Jesus in a place where he had to make a decision to walk away from his destiny and disobey his Father's instructions for him *or* to continue to walk in obedience to God's will for his life, a will which ultimately meant he had to give up his life. Like Jesus, we must constantly live in obedience. Daily obedience!

Disobedience brings about sin - sin brings death

I love the words of Romans 5:12-16 (KJV) which states that Adams disobedience allowed sin to enter

---

[4] Luke 22: 39-46 KJV

into the world whilst Jesus' obedience allowed righteousness to flow into the world. Like Adam, if we continue to live in disobedience to God, whether it's a certain lifestyle, a certain relationship that God wants us to get rid of, a certain job that he wants us to leave which we refuse, whatever it may be, disobedience brings about sin and Romans 6:23 further goes on to tell us that "the wages of sin is death".[5] That is to say that sin comes at a price. It costs us a currency. And that currency is death - sin will cost us our lives. Living a lifestyle of rebellion will cost us the death of our spiritual life, our purpose and our destiny.

What is rebellion?

Rebellion is anything at all that God has told you personally not to do that you are you doing. We can even be rebellious through "well doing". I'll give you my own example. After completing my law degree I knew God's will for my life was not for me to go to law school and become a high flying lawyer as I had wished. But oh my, was this difficult! I tried to bargain with God, I cried, I fretted and everything else in between. The pressure placed on me after completing my degree was simply a lot. When you complete a law degree everyone

---

[5] Romans 6:23 KJV

automatically assumes you are a lawyer and are simply waiting for you to complete the journey, it's like all eyes are on you. Pride and shame almost wants to make you go ahead and just complete the legal journey to prove you could do it and to gain the title etc. I sure had the ability and could have gone ahead and done just that, but had I done so I would have been walking in rebellion. Though I would have lived a life of helping others through the Law, had others look at me as a great person who is a Christian, a lawyer etc I would have known deep in my heart that I was living a rebellious lifestyle, not walking in the path that God had carved out for me but walking in the path which I had created to fuel and feed my pride and to please others. I encourage you not to live your life to please others, but to live your life to please God alone so that you don't miss your purpose and your destiny all together. Of course it will be difficult saying yes to God because saying yes to God usually means saying no to all the other voices around you including your own, but say yes anyway. Go His way anyway. Stick with Him anyway. I guarantee you He'll never leave nor forsake you. I can share with you that it was definitely difficult to watch other people go off to law school, embark on masters, start their careers etc, but I knew deep within me what the Lord was saying to me and that my path was different. It wasn't less than and it wasn't more than... it was just different.

I hope this chapter has helped you to see that making up your mind to be obedient to God is the very first step to allowing you to begin the journey of birthing the true you in the delivery room that is the father's presence. Whatever it is God is saying to you today say yes to Him and allow Him to take you on a journey of self-discovery, or rather God discovery. Learn about him whilst you learn about you. In the next chapter we will deal with the spirit of rejection and how that affects many of us from moving on and birthing the true us. I hope you will continue to read on with me and stay on this journey of healing.

> *The next chapter's about to get deep Sis...but He is your strength...you can do this...*

The Delivery Room

CHAPTER 3

THE STINK OF REJECTION

You're still here! I'm glad!

In this chapter I feel very strongly led to speak on the issue of rejection. I have heard this term many times and it has often been identified as the root cause of many problems in the lives of believers.

I believe that the spirit of rejection acts as the reason why many, men and women alike, find it difficult to truly give birth to their true self. Well in this delivery room there's no shame that's too great, no past that's too dirty for you to bring out and have God deal with. So whilst you're here in the delivery room why not deal with the issues of rejection in your life? The first step of realizing whether rejection has or is affecting you in your life is by analyzing the things that have happened in your life leading up to this point. Now it's not a fact to say that this list is pure truth however these are some ways that the spirit of rejection can enter into a person's life. Many people who have been through any form of abuse, whether it be sexual, physical or verbal abuse, are often prey for this spirit. However, this spirit can also find entry into people's lives by even less traumatic events. One that springs to mind can be issues such as sibling rivalry. Another can be issues such as a relationship ending badly or having alcoholic parents, being rejected by someone of the opposite sex, being rejected into a particular position. These are just but a few examples, but there are of course many more instances. This spirit can enter a person's life in just a single moment; for example, it only takes for someone to say a few hurtful words to you to make you feel rejected. Rejection could come from issues at the work place, in school from classmates, teachers, neglect from parents, knowing that you are an adopted child, being the only one of your sex in a particular place, whatever the case, the spirit of rejection is constantly roaming around looking for the perfect moment to enter into a person's life.

How do you identify the spirit of rejection?

To identify the spirit of rejection it is important to look at your mental state. One of the symptoms of someone suffering from the spirit of rejection is resentment for authority. There is often ill feeling towards those who they believe to be in a position to tell them what to do or how they should behave. When told these things there is often a spirit of offence that comes upon this individual and they feel that they are being made to feel inadequate or unworthy. For this reason there tends to always be a strong need for approval and this person is constantly second guessing their self. They are unable to be their true self and every decision they make is with the intention of gaining praise from others. When this praise is not received they feel condemned and begin to plot their next move to gain approval. This can lead to acts such as spending excessive money to impress others, being over talkative to gain the attention of others, constantly complementing others to manipulate out of them the approval that is been sought. However, at the other end of the spectrum you may get sufferers of the spirit of rejection who are the complete opposite. They completely shut down and put up guards. They build an, "I don't need nobody, I can do it all by myself attitude". This sufferer hates to ask for help and is adamant on never wanting to ask or owe anyone anything. "as long as I do everything myself, no one can hurt me or accuse me of not being good enough, but most importantly if I don't give myself to anyone, no one can have the opportunity to reject me." This sufferer may be the worst of the two. Why? Because the first sufferer of this spirit tends to be aware that they have a problem. However, the 2nd sufferer refuses to accept they have a problem and finds it very difficult to open up to anyone including God. Not to say being either one of these is a good thing but it is important to diagnose oneself and be aware of your specific problem before being able to deal with it. It is one thing to know that you suffer from the spirit of rejection, but it is another to know exactly how it affects you. Think about it, many people suffer from cancer, but you don't just want the doctor to tell you that you have cancer; you want to know what type of cancer you have, breast cancer, bowel cancer, cervical cancer? Identifying your exact problem then marks the start of your recovery plan. Someone suffering from breast cancer has a completely different recovery plan to someone suffering from cervical cancer although they both have cancer. It is fundamental to know exactly what type of rejection you have suffered and exactly how it has affected you and then and only then can you begin your recovery process.

In this chapter I will identify the different types of rejection sufferers and together we will see what category you may fit into and come up with a rejection get well plan to help you set up a recovery process so that you can truly get to that place of enjoying your delivery.

> *Sis try and see which one best describes you (or the old you), you might not tick every box but some of the things may describe you? Be open and be true...you can do*

this… I had traits of all of them by the way, but probably the fan the most…

Rejection Sufferer type 1: The Hanger!

This type of sufferer is often seen in the form of those that have been abused in anyway. This sufferer will have often found that the spirit of rejection entered into their life from an early age. They often find themselves looking for approval from others and have had a pretty unenjoyable childhood. They often suffer from bouts of acute depression but consider themselves a victim. This sufferer if female is often excited at the thought of marriage and would have lived half their life as married in their mind. They have a tender heart and are often very easily hurt. I call them the hanger as they tend to always hang on to other people, especially males. They hang on to the approval of others to help better themselves. They tend to be individuals that suffer from low self esteem and are without a shadow of a doubt over thinkers. Everything must be analysed and again over analysed. This causes this individual to often add 2 and 2 together and come up with 5. Everything tends to be overblown with this individual and when attention is not gained they believe that they have done something wrong or that they are not liked or wanted. When in actual fact it is this spirit at work. This individual may often find it hard to build meaningful and deep relationships and therefore suffer from times of loneliness. In keeping with a hangers characteristic this sufferer often finds the need to take on the issues of others and often finds themselves carrying immense excess baggage which could lead them to breaking point. Like a hanger this sufferer often feels that they are just left on the shelf and are only good for this purpose of convenience and hidden away in a cupboard.

The Hanger needs: What this sufferer craves for is the spirit of adoption. They therefore are in great need of the Holy Ghost as it is only by God's Spirit that this individual can begin to see the affirmation of God in their life.

Hanger's get well plan: This sufferer needs to purge themselves from all areas of unforgiveness towards anyone that has ever done them wrong. They need to begin to delve into God's word regarding the issue of unforgiveness as this in itself is classed as a sin in God's eyes. They need to build a good relationship with someone that can act as a spiritual authority for them, such as a pastor or church elder or maybe even a trusted friend. This individual must feed on scriptures that constantly declare God's love for His children and pray constantly for the affirmation of God's love towards them. In doing this through the power of the word and prayer God's love will begin to transform this individual from a sufferer to an overcomer. Remember, God's word tells us in Revelation 21:4 that "he will wipe every tear from your eyes. There will be no more death, mourning, crying or pain, for the old order of things has passed away"

Rejection Sufferer type 2: The Remote Control!

This sufferer is constantly on auto pilot, and is often those who carry a spirit of rejection because of an ordeal such as rape, or a more sinister form of torture at the hands of another. It is not usually those who endured years of a bad situation, but it is often caused by one traumatic event that changed everything in that person's life. This event is always in the back of this person's mind and they may find it extremely difficult to talk about; in fact some people in this category may have almost convinced themselves that it did not happen. This individual is almost robotic in their way of living, fuelled with the motivation of refusing to be a victim. Unlike the hanger who longs for interaction and approval from others, this sufferer creates their own little world giving access to no one else. They tend to be driven individuals but this ambition is suppressed heavily by fear. This individual hates to ask others for anything or owe others something in fear of being in debt to another. They often fear others and environments, and are likely to fear the dark. They appear to be cold individuals and always hold an element of mystery about them to those around them. This fear of being open is often mistaken for arrogance. Without the intervention of Christ and this individual dealing with the spirit of rejection in their life they are more than likely to settle for a lot less than what God had planned for their life. Their "lone soldier" mentality meant that they always went "solo" and never learnt to give their hearts and trust to anyone. It is likely that this individual therefore invites in the spirit of bitterness and envy. They see what others have and desperately want it but never want to "ask" for anything! They are 100% headstrong about wanting to make their "own" way in life when we are clearly not our "own" but of him who made us. Interestingly enough I came across a television programme the other day that spoke on the issue of the "naked" truth behind the porn industry. It turns out that over 75% of women in this trade were either violently raped or sexually abused in some way during their childhood. It suddenly hit me that it is more than likely that these women are sufferers of the Remote Control form of the spirit of rejection. In order to shut out what happened to them, never wanting to talk about it or open up, they turn to the porn industry for comfort and making lots of money is just a way of ensuring that they never "need" to ask anyone for anything. They are lone soldiers and although they are being torn apart on the inside they are constantly on the go and never stop for a moment to actually take the time to firstly admit what happened to them, and secondly to deal with the issue. The remote control often appears to be controlled by batteries, i.e., lacks the display of emotion and finds it impossible to show emotion to close friends and especially family members.

The Remote Control needs: The remote control needs God the Father. This individual is in desperate need of affirmation and needs the Father's love in order to begin the process of healing. They are in desperate need of the Father's love as they often have felt, "if God loved me, why would He let that happen to me?" This individual needs to begin to recognise God as their saviour and not the reason behind what they encountered. Most importantly this individual needs the Father to step in and reveal unto them who they really are. They have never met the true them! The moment that incident occurred they lost their identity (although in all honesty if they did not know the Father before the incident then they never had true identity). They can't even begin to imagine what they used to be like prior to that event and need the Father to reveal onto them who they really are behind the mask that they have worn since that dreaded day. Remember that in Genesis God declared that he made us in His image. When you give your all to the Father and find out who He is then you find who you are as you were to be His exact reflection.

Remote Control's get well plan: This individual as with the Hanger must find someone to completely open up to and release all that has been held within. If you are in a situation where that is impossible because you have no one of the sort simply ask God to send someone to you and he sure will (seeking professional counselling is one way). This individual must then begin a detox of pride and put aside all guards and let the Father in. From here the Father will do what He does best and turn what the devil meant for bad into good concerning your life. It is also important that this individual begin to note this experience as their testimony. Despite it happening, you are still here!

**Rejection Sufferer type 3:
The Table!**

This sufferer often allows themselves to be used and abused by others. They are often simply a convenience for others and never allow themselves to be more than an object for others to place their "stuff" on. They are often the seen but not heard, although at times their presence may even be drowned because they have been overshadowed by the load that is placed on them. This individual is often swept over by insecurity and tends to have a very quiet persona. The events that led to the entry of the rejection spirit has led them to go into a shell. They constantly suffer from self doubt and unlike the remote control they are always looking for someone to help them. They are afraid of being alone and always need accompaniment in all they do. They fail to use their own resources and realise the anointing on their life because they never feel able and adequate so cling to the anointing of others. This individual runs the risk of placing themselves in a situation where they are repeatedly used by others. Their "I'll say nothing" personality means that other people are left to often make decisions for them and they simply go along with it. They are often followers in life and never take charge of their own decisions. This immensely affects their spiritual walk as they always wait for the prompting of others and never hear what God is saying to them. They don't trust or believe that they can hear from God but are only too eager when someone else has a word for them from God. This sufferer never tends to explore the world but simply stays where they are put. They will never move unless someone prompts them by fully taking them along. You can often recognise this sufferer as the silent tag along friend.

The Table needs: the Table needs a companion. This individual needs the presence of the Holy Ghost in their life. She needs Him to be her friend and comforter.

Table's get well plan: This sufferer needs to let go of all she has held unto and pour out her heart to God. She needs to begin to exercise her friendship with the Holy Spirit on a daily basis. She too needs a confidante that she can speak to about the goings on in her life. She needs to meditate on the scriptures of God and battle the issue of depression through binging on worship and literally snacking during the day on prayer. Worship will break all strongholds with the accompaniment of prayer. This individual often has a purpose concerned with public speaking. How ironic! God will call you to become that very thing you thought you could never do.

Rejection Sufferer type 4: The Fan!

This sufferer has always felt rejected but not due to one particular incident. They have not had years of abuse or torment and they cannot even say why they feel rejected, they just do! The truth is many events have all added up along this sufferer's life to lead to them feeling rejected. Little things such as classmates' comments, parents not giving enough attention, overly strict parents, not feeling pretty enough, skinny enough, curvy enough, too tall, too short, too dark etc have all added up and the spirit of rejection has simply built up bit by bit within this individual. They are the Fan because they strive to be larger than life. They crave to be the centre of attention and are very "in your face" type of people. They appear exceptionally confident and may even be the jokers of the class, making everyone believe they must be a well balanced individual. They are very loud and always desire to be noticed. They are very fast paced individuals, always here there and everywhere and may even be the popular kid.

The Fan needs: The fan needs God to intervene and calm the storm. Their life is one big show and they are in desperate need to know that it is perfectly fine to be who you are and you need not be the centre of attention. They need the Father's love and require God's attention for them to lose the need for attention from others. They must come to the realisation that God has always had them on His mind and has never forgotten them, as this individual often feels that "everyone is blessed and happy but me".

Fan's get well plan: The Fan needs to go into the secret place with God and truly find that love that they are craving from others from the Father himself. They simply need to pray for God's agape love to become real in their life. To know that they are pretty enough, lovely enough, smart enough and everything enough to do and be exactly what God has called them to.

Rejection Sufferer type 5:
The Ruler!

Miss Plastic Fantastic! Similar to the Fan there may not be one event in particular but a collection of small occasions have led to the entry of the rejection spirit. This sufferer constantly hides behind a talent. This may be their looks, their ability to sing, dance, write, sports, educational ability, whatever it may be, they hold onto this dearly and this becomes their identity. They find it hard to show an inch of emotion and tend to always believe that they are right. They are very competitive individuals and would work themselves to the ground to simply prove a point.

The Ruler needs: To know that they are accepted in the beloved. They also need to realise that man may be impressed with talent but the Lord cares about the heart. The ruler is in dying need of love.

The Ruler's get well plan: This love can only be attained from the Father. The Ruler needs to read and digest every single scripture that speaks on the Father's love. This will lead the ruler to understand that they cannot earn God's love but they are already accepted. They will now be able to use their talent and ability or maybe even beauty to glorify the Lord and do His work rather than for the previous purpose of gaining merit from others and taking credit for themselves. The Ruler must understand that all the glory belongs to God and God alone; He never has and never will share his glory with any of us.

These are but only a few types of sufferers and of course there may be many more. Each has in common a desperate need for Love. Well God is love and what better place to go and get love than from a source who is love in himself. God's love is unconditional and he loves you no matter what. No sin could ever take away the love that God has for you. In **Romans 8:35-39** we read *"Who shall separate us from the love of Christ? [shall] tribulation, or distress, or persecution, or famine, or nakedness, or peril, or sword? As it is written, For thy sake we are killed all the day long; we are accounted as sheep for the slaughter. Nay, in all these things we are more than conquerors through him that loved us. For I am persuaded, that neither death, nor life, nor angels, nor principalities, nor powers, nor things present, nor things to come, Nor height, nor depth, nor any other creature, shall be able to separate us from the love of God, which is in Christ Jesus our Lord."* Also **John 3:16** tells us that, *"For God so loved the world, that he gave his only begotten son, that whosoever shall believe in him, shall not die but have eternal life."* Well God doesn't want this eternal life to be one that is full of rejection or the stink of rejection. Remember that Christ was rejected when he came to earth. **John 1:11** tells us that *"he came to that which was his own, but his own did not receive him"*. **Isaiah 53:3** also tells us that *"he was despised and rejected by men, a man of sorrows and familiar with suffering. Like one from whom men hide their faces, he was* *despised and we esteemed him not."* God knows exactly what it is like to be rejected so it is his will for you to be healed from this foul spirit. Believe it or not rejection stinks! Those around you can smell it from a mile off. With the power of the Most High this stink can be shifted. Let go and let God in and give yourself permission to be birthed in his presence. Give God access to clear the stink of rejection from your path to delivery. In the next chapter we will speak on battling loneliness which will further help us along in our quest to birthing the true us and helping us in our healing process. I pray you continue to read on with me.

> *Deep stuff right Sis? Which one did you identify with the most?...And I hope you prayed! And if you didn't pray then pray now? God can help and He will help...just ask him.*
>
> **a massive and a very long hug to you Sis* You're doing this!*

The Delivery Room

CHAPTER 4

BATTLING LONELINESS

Hey there! Glad to see you're back. In this chapter we will focus on loneliness because putting it simply, this is something that many people struggle with, and it's something we so very much need to focus on. In this chapter I would strongly like to advise you to learn to find the joy in being alone. When going through a healing process or a process of finding and birthing the true you this is definitely something you will simply have to get used to.

Why?

God likes to work with us in private (please note, not secret but private). He is very much a private God who deals with us on a one to one personal level. He is a God who delights in intimacy and when he is taking you through a process of changing your mindset and or mending your heart, he likes to do this with minimal intervention from others. Now, don't get me wrong God will certainly put some people in your path that he will allow to act as an aid and an outlet for you to pour your heart out to and to help you along, but you must keep in mind, only God can help, only God can mend, only

God can restore and only God can set free. No pastor, friend or family member can do these things for you, only God has the ability to do this. He may simply put helpers on your path to delivery, but all the glory belongs to our God.

Enjoy your own company

One of the best ways to overcome the feeling of loneliness is not what many of us tend to do. As females, when the feeling of loneliness creeps in we tend to run to a friend, a member of the opposite sex, organise family days etc. However, when God is taking you through a healing process, a recovery or discovery of any kind learning to enjoy your own company is key. I always say that none of us are born knowing exactly who we are. We must get to know ourselves the same way that we would get to know a new friend. You have to take the time to take yourself out, go to lunch with yourself, go to the movies with yourself, spend the evening in with yourself, go shopping with yourself, leave the dog at home and go for a walk with yourself, go on holiday with yourself if you can afford to, whatever way you do it, you must carve out time in your life to spend some time with you.

I was so pleased the other day when my mum came home a little later than she stated she would. When she returned home I asked what she wanted for dinner and she stated she had already taken herself to Nando's and "treated herself". This was rather shocking because my mum rarely treats herself and by herself. It made me feel so good to hear her say that because I thought "good for you!" I believe this is the same way God feels when he see's us spending time with ourselves and getting to know the real us!

Benefits of alone time

One of the benefits of your alone time is that God can truly begin to show you the things that he needs to work on in your life. Sometimes in life, especially in the times we're living in, we have so many distractions and so many things to keep us occupied. With smart phones and social networking sites we're constantly pulled away from alone and quiet time. I can't stress enough how important this is for your delivery. If after reading chapter one you decided to be obedient to God on your pathway to delivery I warn you, do not be surprised when it begins to appear that friends and those you thought would be in your life forever begin to leave. God has a way of stripping us bare and removing people out of our lives so that He can focus on working with us alone. Many times God may want to work on that person alone also and so for both your benefits he causes a separation. The worst thing you can do is run after these things and bring back into your life people that God has ordained their leave. It's so strange because the very thing or people that we think are best for us God often says are not. The bible tells us in Isaiah 55:8 that His ways are not our ways. I remember speaking to God one day and he allowed me to see that often whatever I think it is – it's not, and however I think it is, - it's usually not. His ways are truly not our ways. As human beings when we feel lonely at times we think "let me get some friends, let me do this and that", but God says those lonely periods are the best periods to get to know him by enjoying our alone times. It is often been said that alone does not mean lonely. How true that is. Now, we all know what God said to Adam in Genesis when he said "it is not good for man to be alone".[6] So many people take this scripture and use it or rather twist it as a reason to embark on relationships. I believe when God said this it was only after he had given the man Adam instructions; He had given him purpose and an identity. Adam was whole when he was given a spouse. So many of us because we refuse to get to know ourselves and allow God to work on us in quiet times end up entering into relationships as broken people with an identity crisis. We have an

---

[6] Genesis 2:18 KJV

identity crisis because we don't know who we are. We are broken because we never went to the Potter to get mended. I speak to my wonderful young females especially: allow God to fix you, prune you and to make you whole. If you enter into a relationship whole you will save yourself so much heartache, because I guarantee you, any relationship entered into broken will leave you even more broken when it ends. But a whole woman will bring life and joy to a relationship, wisdom and love.

Do not be afraid

I'm reminded of Ruth and her story in the bible. What an amazing woman. Ruth followed Naomi to a place she did not know, she could have gone like Orpah did and go on to find herself another man. But Ruth wasn't afraid to be alone. Her focus lie in doing what God wanted her to do at the time which was to follow her mother in law. In Ruth's obedience and lack of fear of singleness (because remember Naomi had already declared I have no more sons for you to marry)[7] God was able to bless her. She received a great man in Boaz through her wholeness, lack of fear, and having the ability to be alone. It is so very important that we're able to not be afraid to stand alone.

---

[7] Ruth 1:11-12 KJV

I hope that in this chapter you have been able to see the benefits of alone time and that you are now no longer afraid of being alone. In the next chapter we will deal with relationships because as young women this is one of the very things that stop many of us from birthing our true self in Christ. I pray you will read on with me....talk to you on the other side

CHAPTER 5

DON'T GIVE AWAY GOD'S AFFECTION

Now in this chapter I will be speaking about something that many of us do much too often, especially females. In our quest for love or the perfect idea of romantic bliss, we give away the affection that is due unto God away to another. We do this when our desire for something else becomes greater than our desire for God and the intimacy we ought to have with Him. Recently I have found myself so bugged down with the idea of romance, weddings, marriage and being in a relationship that I have definitely been guilty of allowing my affection to be given away to another. Although there was no one physically there getting my affection I was giving my attention and affection away to an idol. That idol was my thoughts, my feelings and my ever so strong desire for love from a human being. Now don't get me wrong, we all need love, God himself said that it was not good that we be alone, but that love must be given as a gift unto us from God the Father and at the right time. It is not something which we ought to appropriate into our lives ourselves, lest we risk falling victim of self destruction. Now every so often in life we will (without doubt) find ourselves placing something or someone or the thought of something or someone above our desire for God and a lifestyle of intimacy with Him. It is important to know and understand when this happening so that we are able to put a stop to it and return back to our 1st love. I'll list a few ways in which we can be sure to spot when we are edging God out of 1st place in our lives.

Beware of idolatry

God instructs us in the scriptures to never have any other gods apart from him.[8] He warns us of idolatry and the dangers of putting anything before him. Well I believe one of the ways we gain idols is when we find ourselves looking for approval from a source other than God. For example, in the world we live in today many girls desire to be outwardly beautiful. But the only thing is the perception of beauty is forever changing. Now I do keep in mind this is supposed to be a "Christian" book but let's be candid. Once upon a time a big butt was beautiful, now some people don't perceive that as such anymore (some still do), once upon a time big lips were horrid, now we have women in Hollywood and beyond racing for lunchtime quick fix lip filler injections. My point is, whatever was once beautiful

---

[8] Exodus 20:3 KJV

soon won't be viewed as such by the majority in time to come. But when we look to things such as the media or the latest fashion blogs or look to our peers for the definition of beauty and to gain credit as being "beautiful" we've already created an idol for ourselves and have already fallen guilty of giving away Gods affection unto another. Our only true source of our definition of beauty should come from the Lord and he states that we are wonderfully and fearfully made (Psalm 139:14 KJV).

Fitting God into a schedule

Another way we can be sure to spot when we are giving God's affection away to another is when we find ourselves fitting God into our schedule. I think this is definitely one of the ones that most people struggle with. It's so easy to get into the routine of working 9-5, having a lot of studying to do, travelling to business meetings, planning your future, cooking and cleaning and taking care of the kids etc that we can so easily begin to edge God out. Many people find themselves at work from the early morning to the early evening, return home to cook, are absolutely shattered and end up going straight to bed. Most people often do this from Monday to Friday, use their Saturday to recuperate and if Christian, attend a service on Sunday morning, giving God 2 hours of their time in an 168 hour week. However, I guess the question is, are those 2 hours even given to God or are they given to a church service? It would be a very silly thing to presume that attending church on a Sunday morning is you spending time with God, in essence you are spending time with people who just like you, may think they too are spending time with God. Now, don't get me wrong, fellowship is important, but we must be wise in understanding that church allows us fellowship with other believers and it is not a substitute for intimate time with God (keeping in mind that without intimate time alone with him we will never see true and everlasting changes in our lives, and we will never truly come to know God). If you have found yourself in a situation where you are "fitting" God in, please be aware that already you have entered a zone of idolatry, placing importance of things or people over him. I can guarantee you, it's better you have a job which pays you less, a messy house, miss friendship gatherings etc if it means you spend more time with him. I will discuss this in more detail a little later on in the chapter.

Becoming controlling over people or things

This one is another one that most of us fall victim to at one stage or another. Relationships can be and sure are a blessing, however if we are not careful we can so easily get into a place where we begin to control the things and the people around us. When we do this we are sure to be in a place where God is not our number one. Being controlling is a sign that we feel the need to have everything our way, everything on our terms, and it is a clear sign of avoiding submission to God. It can at times also be a sign of fear of losing control and losing the people or things closest to us. However, all of this only happens when we get to a place of forgetting that God is always and forever in control if we allow him to be in our lives. If you have found yourself in a position where you notice that you are controlling, whether through manipulation or emotional blackmail, the people or the situations around you, you need to be aware that you have entered into a zone where you have edged God out of your life. It's also important that you are careful to admit this controlling nature to yourself and submit the core reasons behind the control over to God. I say this because control and manipulation I learnt are clear signs of a witchcraft nature. I think many of us view witchcraft as potions and or night time spookiness (I know I sure did) however, God has taught me that witchcraft can better be described as trying to control situations or people which you have no business or right to control. Now that's deep for a few reasons. Firstly, it shows me that witches are not necessarily people who leave their bodies at night but a witch can also be me! Wow!

Whenever we attempt to control people or control things that are simply none of our business we must be very careful as we have entered into witchcraft territory, manipulating and controlling others. Now how are some of the ways we can do this in everyday life? Well firstly, a simple one is the law of relationships. A good friend of mine describes that when more than two people are in a relationship that is witchcraft. This can mean anything from you trying to come in between two friends, trying to come in between a couple, trying to come in between your parent and one of your siblings, or worse still trying to come in between someone and God. Should this become a perpetual habit, unfortunately habits become our character, and therefore we run the risk of being a witch full stop! That's so deep it scares me and I'm the one writing it!

May we never get to a place where we become so afraid of losing things or people that we come into a lifestyle of manipulation and control and push God out of our lives.

A few ways to ensure you keep him 1<u>st</u>....

Now, there are a few ways to ensure that we do not

edge God out and give his affection away to another. It's important to keep in mind that the God we serve is a gentleman who will never fight us for our time and affection; He'll simply wait patiently until we decide to come back around.

I'd like to detour for a quick second and share a song with you. It's a beautiful song by a man called George Huff titled "You know me". When I first heard the song I was moved to tears because of the beautiful lyrics, they perfectly describe how God patiently waits for us when we have diverted our attentions away from Him. Here are the lyrics below:

You know me everything I do
You know me I'm a window you see through
When all the world is not at home your waiting for
me at the door
And you let me in
Its all beautiful

When I stumble you bruise when I hurt myself it
hurts you
So when I make you cry it makes me never want to
fall again
But the smaller I am the larger your love

You know me everything I do

You know me I'm a window you see through
The most foolish thing I could ever do
Is think that I could lie to you
And put up walls you'd see through them

'Cause you know me you know me you know the
secrets and the scars
That's how into me you are 'cause you know me

In a street full of noise it's amazing how you can
still hear my voice
And when I pull away you care enough to patiently
wait
'Till I come back around like I am now
It's beyond beautiful

'Cause you know me you know me you know the
secrets and the scars
That's how into me you are 'cause you know me

I'm a window you see through
When all the world is not at home
you know the secrets and the scars
That's how into me you are 'cause you know me[9]

---

[9]**http://www.azlyrics.com/lyrics/georgehuff/youknowme.ht ml**

Stay connected to the vine (involve him in your 9-5)

In John 15: 5[10] Jesus states that He is the vine and we are the branches, whoever remains in him will produce much fruit and apart from Him we can do nothing at all. This is very true. But the question then beckons; how do we ensure we stay connected to the vine at all times? Well, one of the ways we can do this is by making sure to include God in the everyday things that we do. I spoke earlier on the dangers of fitting God into a Sunday morning because we're busy with work 9-5, cleaning or cooking or holding business meetings etc. Now, it's important to understand that God is a God that understands practicality. He knows that you have to work in order to pay the bills, He understands that you need to have your meetings in order to keep your business afloat, He gets that the kids need to eat so you have no choice but to cook and clean, He also gets that you're young and need to see your friends and talk to your boyfriend often, He gets it! However, we now need to get it too. We need to understand that God is not asking us to live a "boring" life, a life where all we do is "God, God, God" 24/7 and lose all sense of humanity. He expects quite the opposite in fact. Jesus stated that

---

[10] John 15:5 KJV

He came that we may not only have life but have this life more abundantly![11]   The truth is that God wants your undivided attention so that He can bring you peace, love and joy and this abundant life that His son died so that you can have. He wants nothing more than to have a love walk with you where He is able to love you and vice versa. Going back to our ever so busy schedules, I wonder if you've thought of what your day could be like if you allowed God access into your everyday life? From experience I can share the following with you. Whilst studying for exams whilst at Uni (College for some) I often found myself less in communication with God than I normally would have been. When I got a new job He certainly took the back seat because I placed Him there, I simply "didn't have much time". I'm not too sure when it happened but along the way He started to show me how different my days could have been and could still be when I and if I, instead of looking to fit Him into places or making him wait for me to finish a task before communicating with Him, could allow him to *lead* my day. Cut a long story short this began to happen and I certainly began to enjoy my days a lot more than I ever had done. He began to show me little things during the day to make me laugh (things I would have previously overlooked), He helped me to plan my

---

[11] John 10:10 KJV

time, instead of rushing to get to a destination He made sure I had enough time to get to where I was going by waking me up a little earlier, this way Him and I had valuable talking and "taking things in" time during my travel. He helped me to look at things that would have usually irritated me and ruined my day differently in order for me to have continuous peace and joy. For example, it would only have taken for something not to go to plan for me to flip and think "great, my day is ruined", however, as long as I was willing and obedient to His leading and His correction He would offer me an alternative to how I would have usually reacted. For example He could say "it's ok, it's not that much of a big deal, we'll do it this way instead". As long as I listened and obeyed His voice I found that it truly was no big deal and I could keep my peace and joy even though things had not gone how I planned them.

I hope you're getting the picture I'm trying to paint here. My main point is that no matter how "busy" we are in life we can (if we are willing) have a beautiful and constant relationship with God. If we are willing and obedient and give Him permission to enter into our lives He will lead and guide our everyday lives and become the master of our days. However, it's important to keep in mind, if you are going to allow Him to be the master of your life, it's all or nothing. Sure at the start of your relationship with Him He may allow all things to flow your way to build a foundation with you, however, as time goes on and you grow in Him the time will come when He begins to ask you to do things you may not understand, you may feel is unnecessary or you may simply just not want to do or are too scared to do. On the other side of your constant obedience however, lies the goodness of the land. Remember, God says in Isaiah 1:19 that if you are willing and are obedient, you shall eat the good of the land![12] If you're anything like me you're probably thinking that sounds good but what is the goodness of the land? I can't say I'm 100% sure what the answer to this is, a part of me thinks what is "good" could differ from person to person depending on what you see for your future, however, we can be rest assured that if God says its good, then whatever it is, it's bound to be incredible. ☺

<u>Create an atmosphere conducive for God to remain in!</u>

Another way of ensuring that we are keeping God first place is by creating an atmosphere fit for Him to remain in. Now, instantly I'm sure some may revert to thinking of playing worship music or attending services and watching sermons etc. As

---

[12] Isaiah 1: 19 KJV

great as these are, and they sure do help create a
beautiful atmosphere, I'm more concerned with the
atmosphere that we carry within. Keeping in mind
that God lives within us, I find it awfully strange
that many of us attempt to create a relationship with
him through outward happenings, for example,
dressing a certain way to church, not wearing
makeup, playing only a certain kind of music. Now
of course these are all down to personal choice and
with regards to music it is important what we allow
to feed our spirits, however, I'm speaking on
situations where some people believe that outward
appearances and or surroundings is creating an
atmosphere fit for God to live in. We actually have
some people that more or less live in churches 24/7
yet have a bitter and depressive soul. Now this
individual is living in an atmosphere that they
believe is conducive to allowing God's presence in
their life to manifest greatly, but unfortunately God
doesn't live in the church, He lives in us! So when I
speak of an atmosphere conducive for God to
remain in I'm speaking about within you and more
importantly in your heart. It's important to note that
if you are a person full of bitterness, hurt, anger and
or pain you may find it very difficult to have an
everyday love walk relationship with God, He is a
God that is full of love, joy and peace. Now there's
good news, great news in fact! If you are full of
anything other than joy, peace and love, God allows

us to come as we are. You can't fix your heart before going to God, but understand that when you do come to Him He will expect at certain points that you both begin to work on issues in your heart that are hindering a full and complete relationship between you and Him; in essence anything that is blocking your total peace and joy. So, it's ok not to come into Him with an atmosphere that is whole (no one ever has), but it's not ok to remain that way, He wants you totally free so that He can dwell in you and you in Him forever and for all of eternity, living a lifestyle of joy and peace and love, daily! Now, in order for this to happen, when God wants to begin work on the things that are obstructing this from happening, you have to be willing to say yes.

Don't be afraid to say 'Yes'

Please keep in mind that God never forces Himself upon us, He is a complete gentleman. You may have said yes to Him the last 30 times but He will never assume that you will say yes on the 31st time and will always ask your permission before beginning a process of healing of anything within you. Your only job is to say yes. Sounds simple enough, but the reason we have so many hurting Christians is because we are the people most afraid of healing. I guess many people are scared of healing because they know that healing brings up a lot of pain and a lot of heartache that they have kept buried for so long. However, how will you ever get well if you don't allow the operation to take place? There is no quick fix to healing, it often takes a long process, but you can be sure He will be right there with you every single step of the way! On the other side of you saying yes to healing lies a beautiful life full of freedom. The alternative is for you to continue living in the state you are now for the rest of your life or for a lot longer than you need to. So whatever it is you need healing from today, whether it's a painful experience or past, issues of pride, low self-esteem, lack of self-love, whatever it may be...say yes today!

I'd like to end this chapter by reminding you that when we speak on giving God's affection to another, we say it's God's affection because it truly does belong to Him. The bible tells us that we were bought at a price[13] and therefore we do not belong to ourselves. Whatever it is that's getting your attention instead of God I assure you that person or thing would not die for you on a cross with the hope that over 2000 years later you will have a life full of joy, peace and eternal life. God won our love fair and square; our affections and 1st place in our life belong to Him. I'd like to close by sharing another

---

[13] 1 Corinthians 7:23 KJV

song with you which perfectly explains this. It is a
song by Israel Houghton and New breed titled
"You've won my affection".

> *You've won my affection*
> *You've captured my heart*
> *You have my devotion*
> *My worship is yours*
> *You've won my affection*
> *You've captured my heart*
> *Now I am yours*
> *Completely yours forever*
>
> *I see the sacrifice you gave*
> *I know the awesome price you paid*
> *You went the distance*
> *You finished strong*
> *We were your passion*
> *So you gave your all*
> *Now I am yours, completely yours*
> *Forever*[14]

---

[14]http://www.music-lyrics-
gospel.com/gospel_music_lyrics/youve_won_my_affection_1
3510.asp

The Delivery Room

CHAPTER 6

DEATH BY PAPER CUTS

In this chapter we'll be talking about the little things that can add up to lead us to committing our own spiritual death - a death by paper cuts. These little things can come in many forms. From little niggling things we do such as gossip, to bad self perception. Many of us view these things as just "little things" but all of these things can lead us to hindering our own birth in the delivery room. Some of the paper cuts that I am aware of including the following.

Gossip

Yep, it's the one many of us, especially ladies, forever battle with. Our tongues truly need salvation. With the women's ministry that I founded called "Pure Hearts" I remember us having a women's meeting a few months ago and speaking on the issue of gossip. It was funny that God had placed it on my heart to speak on this subject as walking into the room it was already clear that a spirit of division, gossip and or animosity already existed in the room amongst the ladies present. We went on to speak about the subject and it soon became clear that many of us fail to realise that when we gossip we are the true and only victims. I will further go on to explain how and why.

<u>Gossip drains</u>

Ever noticed that gossiping drains you? And I mean physically as well as spiritually. I can remember a time when I came off the phone with a friend after spending almost 3 hours talking about a subject matter which truly was none of our business and the moment I came off the phone I literally felt like I had just ran a marathon. I was sweaty and breathing heavily and felt like I was in a daze. Sounds dramatic but I promise you I kid you not. I remember uttering the words "Abba I'm sorry" whilst trying to hide my face from Him in shame knowing full well that He was not best pleased. Those few hours of self gratification and tearing apart others led to me feeling physically drained and not wanting anymore phone conversations for at least another week, and left me spiritually drained for a few days after that. I felt cut off from God's love because I knew I had not only sinned but gossiped, which meant I had dragged someone else into my sin and they had dragged me into theirs as gossiping takes two. I had to think to myself, "was that even worth it?" "I feel tired and I can't freely go and talk to God because I'm covered in guilt and embarrassment and all of this for a conversation about a subject matter which had absolutely nothing to do with me?" I made my mind up then - it's not worth it. When we gossip we drain ourselves and cut ourselves off and entice others to join us in our sin.

Gossip destroys

Gossip has the power to destroy. I recently heard a pastor say that it takes time to build up trust and relationships and yet it can take but a second to destroy it. I see this as fitting especially in the area of gossip. I've seen so many friendships and sisterhoods destroyed by the act of gossip. Friends that have been on a beautiful journey for years and yet one session of self gratification through gossip can destroy what could have been a long life friendship. They could have been each other's maid of honours, had double dinner dates with their husbands, enjoyed watching their kids grow together and enjoyed family holidays, but gossip destroyed all that could have been. Gossip also has the power to destroy your walk of righteousness with God. If God has been taking time to work on your character and you have been diligent and obedient in the way that He has been teaching you, it's a terrible setback for you when you then allow yourself to be enticed into gossip. You are literally destroying everything that you have been working towards with Him. Gossip also destroys your perception. It affects the way you view the person you have just gossiped with, the way you view yourself and the way you view the subject of the gossip. You begin to notice the level of untrustworthiness and character flaws that lie within your gossip partner, you begin to mistrust them as you truly begin to see that truth lies in the saying "if they gossip with you they will gossip about you". You also begin to dislike yourself as there is no time more appropriate to witness the ugly in you then when you make it your purpose to speak ill and disgustingly about others. Gossip literally destroys all that God is trying to build up in you.

Gossip hinders blessings

This is probably the biggest and most crucial point. Gossip can hinder whatever blessing was on its way to you (sounds super religious I'm sure but it's the truth). Let's take a look at some scriptural examples. I love Matthew 5:9[15] which says "blessed are the peacemakers for they shall be called the children of God". Putting it simply if you are a gossip will you be called a child of God? For the Kingdom of God is righteousness, peace and joy, if you habitually gossip surely you have none of the above? I like to flip scripture on its head sometimes

---

[15] Matthew 5: 9 KJV

and look at what it's not saying through what it is saying. Here's what I mean; if the scripture says "blessed are the peace makers for they shall be called the children of God", surely this means that those that are not peacemakers shall not be called the children of God? Now, this means if you are a gossip which in turn means you are a person who creates anarchy and confusion and does not seek to bring about peace then you are not a peacemaker. We all have the power within us to create peace in any and all situations even when we have been wronged. For example, imagine a friend of yours calls you to inform you that another friend has spoken about you in an awful way, yes you have been wronged and yes you may feel upset and hurt about this revelation, however, your reaction to the information received is key to deciding whether you then allow yourself to fall into sin through another person's sin. Firstly, the person who has spoken about you in a negative manner has sinned, the person who told you about this person's sin has sinned (if they didn't first of all approach the person who made the comments about you and inform them of how they felt before coming to share with you) and lastly if your reaction is then to speak with the informer about the original gossiper and discuss how wrong they were and how awful what they did was etc then you have fallen into sin also. What a mighty mess!

This is such a constant cycle in female friendships that sometimes one person can find themselves being the original gossiper, the gossiped about and the informer of the gossip that occurred, all in the space of one week. How crazy! I would like to take this time to encourage all women, young and old, if you are in a friendship circle which sounds anything like or remotely close to this - leave! It is not an atmosphere conducive to peace, growth, success or God's blessings in your life. You are all simply hindering one another's growth and nothing fruitful can ever fully grow from such toxic ties that many of us call friendships. Jealousy, anger and strife will be the driving force behind these friendships as opposed to love, support and sisterhood. I can share with you that having been in friendship circles before that were fuelled with jealousy and constant backbiting it's the most beautiful thing to have friendships that are now built in and around love. So, in order to avoid gossip start by choosing your friendships well!

> *Most important thing we can do Sis...Ask God to choose your friends for you...*

Bad self perception / Low self esteem

Another area that can contribute to a death by paper

cuts is the area of bad self-perception and or low self-esteem. It seems almost unfair to have this listed here as some may perceive it as entirely different from gossip as that is a sin that you can control whereas this is something that you cannot control? Well we can control our own self-perception and self-esteem, so to remain in bad self-perception and continuously live in low self-esteem I believe is a sin in itself. When we have a poor self-image we indirectly state that God's handiwork is not as perfect as he claimed. This poor self-image can lead to a spiritual death because it begins to hinder us from doing the things that God has called us to do. For example, if we take a look at the book of Exodus, God called Moses to lead the children of Israel out of their oppression in Egypt and into the promise land. However, when God called Moses his reaction wasn't initially "yes lord", his reaction was to say "who am I that I should go to Pharaoh, and that I should bring forth the children of Israel out of Egypt?"[16] That wasn't humility that was complete bad self-perception and low self-esteem. Thank God that He spent time reassuring Moses that he indeed was chosen and could perform all that He had called him to do. Had Moses continued in his unbelief and self-doubt due to bad self-perception this would have concluded to him missing the purpose that

---

[16] Exodus 3:11 KJV

God had called him to; essentially causing him to disobey God, resulting in sin. This is why it is so important that we deal with things such as bad self-perception and low self-esteem as they can cause us a big problem in our walk with God. God tells us that we are "fearfully and wonderfully made"[17] and we can do all things through Christ who strengthens us.[18] A tip that I would give to anyone reading this suffering from low self-esteem or bad self-perception is to face your fears in order to overcome them! For example, if your fear is people and you pray to God for Him to help you overcome this then don't be surprised if more invitations for outings or dinners start to come up. God helps us to overcome our fears by putting us in positions where we are forced to confront them. You will not be healed of fear of people before He makes you face people. He will make you face people, even in your fear, in order to get you healed of the fear. So the next time someone invites you out to dinner, it is God helping you to get healed - say yes and go, and keep on going! Don't allow the little things to keep you from living the wonderful life that God has planned for you on the other side of your fear. ☺

---

[17] Psalm 139:14 KJV

[18] Philippians 4:13 KJV

You're beautiful Sis...and so perfectly perfect just the way you are...

Pride

Another area that would be considered a "little" sin but that could lead to us living out a death by paper cuts is the issue of pride. Now I'm sure when many of us think of pride we imagine a pompous individual with arrogance, or someone who never wants to ask for help and believes they may be better than others. But I want to speak about the pride we have towards our God! It wasn't until recently that I started to realise that I have a prideful attitude towards God. Sounds crazy I know, but I'll explain. My revelation if you like, came when it was time for me to speak at a women's meeting we were holding. I remember being so fearful that I just wanted to call it quits altogether. I remember thinking and saying "I don't want people to be looking at me and focusing on me" and in that moment I felt God look at me as a selfish and prideful individual. This confused me as I felt fear was a valuable enough reason to not want to do something, I wasn't saying no I don't care, no I don't want to, I was simply saying, "I'm scared". But even fear isn't a valuable excuse with God, in fact what He showed me was that the one reason I was afraid was because I was being prideful and selfish and placing all the attention on me. My focus wasn't on Him and whatever He wanted to get across to His people coming that night, my focus was on me and how people would look at me, would they judge me, would they laugh or ridicule me? I was being selfish and prideful and I was in danger of stealing the limelight from God. God had to deal with me about this. He taught me to never allow fear to lead me to a place of self-centeredness and only seeing "me", He taught me that pride, even gained through fear, can lead me to a place of being prideful towards God and what He has called me to do, He taught me to always place the focus on Him and not on me. Pride can amount to you living a life causing you death by paper cuts, eradicate yourself of pride and live a self-less life so much as is pleasing in His eyes!

Pride comes before a fall Sis…let it go…

Refusal to let go of the past

Another thing that could add up to causing us a spiritual death by paper cuts is when we refuse to let go of the past. This is probably the biggest one that I would say keeps many people (especially us females) from moving on to the life that God has set up for us in our future. The first type of refusal that many of us find difficult to let go of is relationships.

It's so crazy to me that many of us still long for and cling to the hopes of a relationship that either died years ago or one that God has made known to us that we clearly should not be in with this particular person in question. My only answer for this level of craziness must be that we don't love ourselves. For a woman to love herself she will be able to let go (although find it hard) of what isn't good for her and look forward to the joys of getting into a relationship that will be good for her. However, many of us will fight and fight some more for that very thing that is clearly hurting us and causing us a crazy amount of heartache.

Many of us women also do this by holding unto the fact that that guy who doesn't want us may want us one day - chances are he won't! But we will still hold on to this belief. Crazy! It's crazy because the only victim in all of this is you! The only person hurting in all of this is you; the only person not moving on here is you. I truly believe that an example of a death by paper cut is worse when we hold on to the past. We literally end up missing out on joy, missing out on peace and missing out on life whilst we remain living in anticipation, false hope, heartache and pain that we are causing ourselves. How can we not love ourselves enough to want the best for ourselves?! You are a daughter of the King and you should indeed behave as such. It's important to remember that whilst you are so very busy holding unto pain and anguish you are refusing to allow yourself to enter into joy and love. It's actually funny that as females when we get ourselves into these kinds of situations we wait and expect God to bring us joy and happiness supernaturally. But more times than none what we actually mean is "God I'll be happy and I'll only be happy if you give me that thing that I want". The problem here is God won't be emotionally black mailed and if something is not good for you He won't give it to you. If you want it you'll have to go and get it yourself, but unfortunately you will also then have to bare the repercussions of that decision, which will, I guarantee you, always end badly and lead you to more heartache than you ever thought imaginable. You see, when God says that something is bad for us it is for our sake. When he blocks roads to certain relationships, it is for our good. Even if you find what you believe to be the best man in the world but he doesn't feel the same way about you, you had better thank your lucky stars because God knows exactly why that didn't work out. The only reason that God keeps the past from entering into our future is to protect us. I describe it like this; imagine driving down a road that seems so clear, there is sunshine and brisk light wind and nothing but joy and happiness in sight, you are driving along and come to a bend in the road to your right and you begin to turn into the road. All of a sudden you are met with a catastrophe, there has been the most awful car crash and there's so much blood on the road it is clear that there are some fatalities, ambulance crews and the police are all over the scene and you cannot believe your eyes. You are shocked that just a few moments ago before you turned into this corner you were enjoying the wind in your hair and loving the feel of the brisk wind. Well life can be just like this. What we perceive as the perfect road can actually lead us to a disaster zone. *But thank God for God!* God can see further than we can see and He has already seen down that bend in the road even before we were formed in our mother's womb, so when God says no to something, trust Him! Believe Him! And obey Him! Because He has seen what lies in the bend in the road, He has gone ahead of you and see's that this road that seems so perfect to you will actually cause you great misery and see's that a disaster lies ahead. What you now need to do is love yourself enough to listen to Him and go in the other direction; the direction that He is leading you to.

Well how will I know if He is saying no?

It's very simple. If something is causing you misery and heartache already, more than it does bring you peace and joy then this is not of God and will lead you down a road to disaster. It is also important to keep in communication with God, pray and pray some more. Pray for God to direct you away from this if it is not for you, pray that He send you confirmation if it is for you and simply do NOT act until He does, no matter how long it takes for you to hear back! Prevention is so very much better than cure people!

> *If he's hurting you then he's not worthy of you Sis...let him go...you can do this!*

With that said, please do not allow holding unto the past and hurting yourself to keep you from the life of peace and joy that God has for you. If it's heartbreak that you are scared of, well keep in mind that many have endured it, you are not so special that you cannot endure it too. Yes it will hurt, yes you will feel lonely, yes you will cry, yes you may have to watch others in relationships and feel sad, but let go anyway! On the other side of your obedience is a good life filled with joy, get rid of the life that you currently know which is daily self-harming of your own heart. Stop living a life of death by paper-cuts through a refusal to let go of the past.

How else may I be refusing to let go of the past?

Many of us may not experience a refusal to let go of the past through relationships, but by actually attempting to live in the past, nevertheless there are benefits to letting go of the past.

Benefits of letting go of the past

I've often heard it said that in order to receive what God has for you; you have to be willing to handover what is already in your hand. This is exactly why it is important that we let go of the past. If you cannot let go of pain, tears and false hope, God cannot bring you peace, love and hope fulfilled. God is willing to bless you with all the good things that you can comprehend and even those that you have never thought of, but He needs you to work with Him; you do the letting go and He'll help you spring clean and then fill you with goodness! Letting go of the past will also mean you can sleep at night! How many of us can honestly say that when our minds aren't settled we can sleep with ease? I can't! There is no better pillow than laying your head on a peaceful and clear mind. So many people go to bed at night waking up with the same anguish and disturbance as the night before and the night before that. Letting go of the past literally means that you can wake up with a clear mind and an uncontaminated view of the day ahead. You are able to see each day as a chance for Gods goodness and his goodness is able to flow into your life without any disturbance from past hurts and or past ties.

You see it's important that we are willing to move on from the past in order to attain the future. I will not lie to you, letting go of the past will be difficult because it is all we have ever known, however, change is good! Change is a catalyst for a new way of living and a new level of joy and peace in our lives. Nothing worth having has ever happened without change. If we take a look at the story of the children of Israel whom God released from the oppressive hands of Pharaoh in Egypt we see why change is for the good but we also see that change is a difficult process. The children of Israel expected to go straight from Egypt into the Promised Land but unfortunately there was a process! They first had to endure the journey through the wilderness where they had to learn to trust God and His promises of good for their future. You see when God wants us to let go of the past He doesn't release us into the future right away, there is often a wilderness period. During this time you can be unsure, uncertain and even like the children of Israel you can wish you stayed where you were and didn't attempt to change at all. However, this process (wilderness) period is needed. It is needed to help you prepare for the future, to help you get rid of any nasty habits that you picked up in the wilderness that may destroy your future and to help you to build a relationship of trust and intimacy up with God as this will sustain you in your future. The wilderness period may make you want to give up but keep on persevering anyway, keep going anyway and keep hoping for the goodness of God anyway.

Now even though I have spoken a lot about relationships concerning the area of letting go of the past please keep in mind this same principle applies to whatever situation that you know that God wants you to let go of. For example, God could be speaking to you about letting go of one job to enter into a new one, He could be speaking to you about letting go of a grudge or unforgiveness that you have always harboured, He could be speaking to you about letting go of negative thoughts about yourself, lying, fornicating, a homosexual lifestyle, doubt, shame, a habit of stealing, laziness and lack of self-control, over eating or an unhealthy lifestyle maybe! Whatever it may be... let it go!

So much more peace lies ahead Sis...you can do this...

90

I will now speak about some ways that we may try to creep back into our lives issues of the past which we have already made a decision to let go of. It is important to know how to avoid this as I have seen many people including myself make decisions only to return right back to square one all over again, make a decision again and return back again....and guess what? Make the decision the final time again and yet....return back to square one again. We fail to realise that all of this just leads to us adding to our own heartache and unnecessarily prolonging the journey to our very own promised land.

How to avoid returning back into the old

Make wise decisions not good decisions

I love this one! I used to be one of those people that made decisions based on the thought process "well it's not bad if I do that", and certainly it's the truth it wasn't bad, but was it wise?! I will give you a more in depth example. Imagine we have a 24 year old girl called Sandra. Now Sandra and her boyfriend Eric have been in a relationship where they have been fornicating for the past few months. Both Sandra and Eric are believers but Sandra takes her relationship with God a lot more seriously than Eric does his, Eric doesn't really mind fornicating. Sandra has known in her heart for quite a while that what they were doing was wrong and was totally out of character for her, if her parents were to ever find out they would be so disappointed in her. Sandra hasn't even told her close friends what's going on because she's so shocked at herself and what she is doing. Following months of living a lifestyle of secret sin she finally decides that her and Eric are to go on a break, naturally Eric doesn't want this. After much breaking up and getting back together she eventually is strong enough to declare that they are officially done. Sandra got herself back into a good relationship with God and repented; she felt spiritually strong and couldn't believe she had even allowed what happened with Eric to take place. She started to give her testimony in church and began to help and encourage other girls to keep themselves pure until marriage. A few months went by and she was shocked to get a call from Eric, he stated that he wanted to come over and have a conversation with her, Sandra felt there wasn't nothing bad in that and so she agreed! Oh boy!

Oh dear Sis! You see here Sandra had already made a terrible mistake and had already set herself up for a big time fall. Sandra's thinking was "there's nothing bad in him coming over to talk", but her thinking should have been "is it wise for me to allow him to come over to see me?! Is it wise for me to be at home alone with this man who I had spent so many months fornicating with? Is it wise for me to allow him to come over knowing full well that feelings and emotions could be stirred up again? Is it wise to put myself in a position where talking could lead to something else? Am I being wise?!"

Proverbs 4:7 explains it so well Sis, "wisdom is the principal thing; therefore get wisdom. And in all your getting, get understanding."

Lo and behold Eric came over and they spoke, speaking led to emotions of old times being stirred up and surely Sandra was back fornicating, her spiritual life back in the mess it was in before.

The lesson to learn from Sandra's story is to understand that once you let something go out of your life do not then put yourself back in a compromising situation no matter how spiritually grown you now perceive yourself to be. No one is infallible! For example, if the guy you were fornicating with is not a changed man he will lead you back into that lifestyle so don't go to his house to "just talk", he shouldn't come to yours to "just talk". Now you may need to speak to him, but how about we think of other ways in which we can make this happen without putting the both of you in a compromising situation. How about a meeting in a local Starbucks? Meet him for drinks? Speak on the phone at a decent hour? There are loads of other options! Let us let wisdom have a say in our lives ladies

Let us pray for wisdom Sis

**Be disciplined*

Here's another important one. Discipline is so very key when it comes to staying free from issues of the past. Discipline to me is doing something that you may not even want to do but do it anyway for the sake of a bigger purpose. If we take an athlete like Usain Bolt for example, we all see him breaking world record after record and we begin to take the bigness of this fact lightly, we start to think well he must just find this thing so easy, but that's not the case. It takes under 10seconds for Usain Bolt to complete the 100m sprint and in the blink of an eye he has made history. However, for those little 10seconds that flashes by so very quickly he has had to endure years of hard work through discipline. He has had to train in extremely hot weather, during cold seasons, on days when he didn't feel like it, days when his body felt like it was giving out on him, days when he had emotional issues going on and days when he just simply could not be bothered.

He would have had to have watched his diet and made sure he was eating right, cut some favourites out and maybe stick to what was good for his body only for a period of time. It was a lifestyle of prolonged discipline that gave him the victories that he achieved in less in than 10seconds of time. Our lives are very similar to this. If God has asked you to give up a particular thing, it is for a greater purpose. For example if God has asked you to give up smoking it is so you can live longer and enjoy seeing your children and grandchildren grow up. But when God asks us to give up something only discipline can ensure we do not fall back into old habits. So how do you get disciplined? Well it's the little things! If you are someone that is failing in school God could tell you to get disciplined in the area of waking up early and making sure you have breakfast before leaving every morning. Sounds like such a little task but it's these little things that could help you to achieve your goal of doing better in school, eating well could very well improve your concentration. If you are an over eater and God wants you disciplined in the area of how much food you eat well get disciplined and tell yourself "I am not allowed to eat past 6pm" and stick to it. If it's an old relationship you need to eradicate get disciplined and say I will not pick up his calls and in fact I may even change my number completely. The only way to ensure we don't fall back into old ways is through this act of discipline, it's all well and good praying about something but exercise common sense in the way you ensure that you don't fall back in. Be a disciplined individual!

*Be accountable

Being accountable is one of the main ways to make sure that you don't fall back into old habits. We all need someone or some people that can pull us up on our crap and tell us how it is. If you have anyone in your life that isn't afraid to tell you when you are wrong, appreciate them! You need them! The danger comes when we have no one to answer to or fall into the delusion of believing "I only answer to God". No! You have to answer to people too, that's why we have parents and authority such as the police and the courts. No man should be a law unto themselves and there must be someone that has an important say in your life. Accountability is particularly key to staying free but you have to be willing to make yourself accountable by being open and honest with those that God has put around you. You cannot go around lying and keeping things from people and yet claiming you are accountable to them, and you cannot expect them to just know what is going on, they are not psychic (I'm so preaching to myself here)! Be open and be honest! For example with our previous example Sandra, I'm sure that as someone that was back in church and took an active role in the church she had people that she was accountable to. She could have called someone and said "listen Eric wants to come over, you know our history which was only a few months ago, what do you think I should do?" But she didn't. She had accountability but she didn't make herself accountable. Big difference! Had she had made a simple phone call maybe just maybe someone would have given her some wisdom to say, I don't think that's a good idea. Now don't get me wrong I am the biggest believer in being independent and not being a spiritual cripple (i.e. leaning on others for guidance 24/7) but I also believe that if you have to sneak about and lie you already should know in yourself that you are entering into a danger zone. So in order to ensure that you stay free of the issues of the past learn to be accountable to someone that you know has your best interest at heart and understands Godly principles! I.e. someone who won't just tell you what you want to hear, cause that my friend is not your friend but an enemy of progress! Proverbs 27:6 "Faithful are the wounds of a friend, but the kisses of an enemy are deceitful"

*** Picture the future (as far as you can see it He'll give it to you.).**

This one is a pretty important one to ensuring you

don't slip back into old habits. It's what I would call the secret to staying away from the past and allowing yourself to keep going forward. It's probably the one I found the most helpful. You see there will always be times when staying away from the past seems impossible, the temptation to fall back into our old ways seems greater than we can resist and greater than the strength to keep on going. Sometimes the only way we can resist past habits is to literally remind ourselves of why we are staying away from it in the first place by picturing the future. This can be achieved by reminding yourself of why sin is obstructive to the future that God has in store for us. Sin hinders our blessings, cuts off our communication with God, covers us in guilt that means we cannot boldly enter into the presence of God, cripples our ability to pray and causes us immense heartache. However, if we abstain from our past sinful nature we are able to boldly go to God, boldly pray and to continue reaching for the purpose and life He has already set before us. The best thing we can do when the past calls therefore is to picture our future. Remember God said to Abraham in Genesis that as far as He could see it, it would be given unto him.[19]

---

[19] Genesis 13:15 KJV

** Love yourself*

This is definitely one that's so very much needed to aid you on your journey forward. Loving yourself so much to want the best for yourself, despite what you may have to endure, including resisting the temptations of the past, is the most precious gift you could ever give to yourself.

Yes leaving the past is hard; yes it will be a difficult journey and at times seem almost impossible to leave behind the life that you have always known and even enjoyed, but loving yourself perfectly and fully will allow you the strength to keep on pushing forward to the life that God has planned out for you in your future, a life full of joy and a peace from God that surpasses all understanding. I promise you, nothing in this world feels better than being able to lay your head on the pillow at night and have no heartache, no regret, no tears, no pain and no brokenness but complete peace and an excitement about the next day to come. Many girls struggle with loving themselves enough to move on, especially when it comes to relationships, but truly, no matter how hard it is, the best thing we can ever do is to love ourselves enough to want the best for ourselves. Put you first! Put your heart first! Put your future first!

You're worthy of peace Sis…we all are!

Pray!

Another big one! Prayer can and prayer will give you that supernatural strength to keep on moving forward and to do so with peace of mind and a level of joy that you never thought imaginable. Prayer will give you access to let in the one person that you need more than anyone else in the world especially during your time of pain and or heartache - God Himself! He is the only one that can turn a mess into a message and dig us out of holes that we dug for ourselves.

Prayer gives God permission and access to be able to help and assist you in making the journey just that much more bearable. Prayer also gives you something to do other than wallow in self-pity, a 30 day prayer at 7am every morning for example, will keep you busy and less idol. But if you're anything like me, when you're feeling down and out is not usually the time that you feel like praying? But notice that word I just used there; "feel". Our feelings or rather our submission to our feelings has a lot to answer for in causing us so much trouble in our lives. We cannot allow our lack of "feeling" like praying to deter us from praying. We need to grow up! Even if the only words we can bring to utterance is "God please help me" just continue to utter those words. You can have many people praying for you yes, but I guess no one can pray for you like you could?

It is also important to not be naive and silly about our situations. Please do not pray yet take no action. Faith without works is truly dead. As well as allowing God access into your situation you also need to allow a level of action by you to be taking place.

I hope that this chapter has helped you to understand that the "little" things are truly what lead to the big bad things happening in our lives. There is no small area of sin as all these "little" things eventually add up to take us under if we are not careful. Writing this chapter certainly helped me to understand that "little" things need to be nipped in the bud otherwise they truly do grow to become untameable beasts in our lives. May our Abba Father help us all in moving away from the "little" things. And if after reading this chapter you have seen that there are some things that you need to do or have not been doing but want to do, I pray He guides you, gives you the strength, the courage, the protection, the wisdom and an open ear to hear Him through the process.

The Delivery Room

CHAPTER 7

KNOWING THE LORD'S VOICE

Knowing the Lord's voice is the most important thing in this world. There is simply nothing else that should take precedent over hearing the Lord's voice and learning to know and recognise that voice. I'm always taken by Jesus' words in John 10:4-5 when He states that His sheep know His voice and the voice of another they will not follow.[20] That confirms to me that there are many voices out there that are vying to gain control over us. If you're anything like me there are probably times when you feel "is that really God or am I just talking back to myself". I felt like this for such a long time. But I can encourage you; the more you talk to the voice of the Lord the more He speaks back to you and the louder and more assured you are in the voice of whom you are hearing.

God's words are true and bring life

One of the ways of knowing who you are hearing from is having the knowledge that God's words bring life and His words bring truth. If you are

---

[20] John 10:4-5 KJV

hearing a voice which constantly tells you "you've sinned, you've messed up, beg me to forgive you, I can't ever use you, you're not as good as her or him", that is not the voice of our God. Jesus proclaimed that He came to bring life and life more abundantly; He also proclaimed that the power of life and death is in the tongue; therefore He wouldn't use *His* tongue to speak deathly words to you and over you. When you hear a voice like that you simply need to rebuke it because it is not our God speaking. Jesus said the devil is the father of lies[21]; well you simply rebuke his lies. Do not entertain that voice by having a conversation with it, rebuke and keep it moving.

<u>Well what voice is God's?</u>

One of the ways we can know the voice of God is to know the heart of God, as out of the abundance of the heart, the mouth speaks.[22] There is no better way to knowing the heart of God, than to know His voice personally for yourself and to have a love walk relationship with Him. However, as this is what we are attempting to do and so many of us may not yet be at that place, we will look at another

---

[21] John 8:44 KJV

[22] Luke 6:45 KJV

way of getting to know the voice of God which is to look at the characteristics of God in scripture which point us to the heart of God. If you believe you are in a place where you are truly hearing and know the voice of God this will still be a great checklist for you in confirming the one you are walking with is truly our God!

God is merciful

One of the ways of being sure the voice you hear is that of God's is if this voice promotes mercy. Our God is a merciful God. In the book of Exodus we see the abundance of mercy which God bestowed on the children of Israel. He continuously provided manna, provided a way in the midst of the sea and even in their moaning and complaining and unbelief God was merciful. If the one you are speaking with encourages you to be merciful unto others this is surely the good and beautiful voice of God.

God is forgiving

Our God is forever forgiving. When the woman in the book of John[23] was caught in adultery and the men of the land wanted to stone her as a consequence of her sin, Jesus' reaction was to teach

---

[23] John 8 KJV

those about to commit a sin themselves to have an attitude of forgiveness and mercy towards someone else's sin. If the voice you are speaking with encourages you to forgive easily and quickly and to keep no record of the wrongs of others, this is certainly the wonderful voice of our God who is a good and forgiving God!

God is fair

Our God is always fair and His fairness can even go against the law and the rules set by man. We see this in the book of Numbers when the children of Israel had finally acquired the Promise Land and it was time for the distribution of the land. Custom had it that land would be given to the men of each household. However, the daughters of Zelophehad had no men left in their blood line to acquire this land on their behalf. It was only right in keeping with the laws of the time and the culture that the daughters of Zelophehad lose their right to their own land because of this. However, on their partition to Joshua, Joshua sought the Lord and the Lord instructed Joshua to give them the land that was due unto them. What a good and fair God we serve! No matter what the law says, what custom or tradition says, the voice of the Lord always steers us to be fair and to do good. He never instructs us to cheat people out of what is rightfully theirs using the law or custom as an excuse. The voice of the

Lord is a fair One!

God is a protector

The voice of the Lord always allows you to know that you are protected. I am reminded of Shadrach, Meshach and Abednego in the book of Daniel who were placed in burning flames in their refusal to worship an idol. The Lord never left them! He was true to His word to be a protector because the voice of our God never lies. The Lord was a protector for them in times of great fear and hardship. The voice of God will always be your protector, guiding you through the fire. Now notice, the Lord didn't make the fire to disappear. Shadrach, Meshach and Abednego sure had to endure the fire but the flames did not harm them because God was with them talking with them and protecting them. God may not clear your fire or your problems, but for His glory He will allow you to go through the fire but the fire will not harm you. The fire will not consume you if you keep your ears open to the voice of the Lord and you keep your eyes fixed on the hill where your help comes from.

God is strong

Our God is a strong God. Now I guess you'll be expecting me to declare that therefore you are strong too? Well yes and no. You are of course strong because He is strong but I say yes and no because your strength in Him only lies in your weakness. The scripture tells us in 2 Corinthians 12:19 that God's strength is made perfect in our weakness. When you attempt to be strong God's perfect strength cannot be made manifest in your life as He will never play a game of battle of the strongest will with you. God will never rival your will. You must simply submit your will and allow His will to be the only will in existence in your life. Your will and his will cannot co-exist. The voice of the Lord will therefore encourage you to not be afraid to be weak in Him. God's voice will encourage you to embrace seasons of weakness in God and to allow God to be the strength in your life and over all things concerning you. The voice of God will not tell you to act as though you have it all together, not to let people see your weaknesses and flaws, the voice of God will rather encourage these things, the voice of God will tell you it's ok not to be ok. The voice of God will cause the arms of God to embrace you in times of weakness, allowing His strength to become perfect in your life.

God is fearless

The voice of God will never cause you to live in fear. God will never tell you something that brings a deep fear in you. Now of course sometimes God may tell you something that you don't particularly want to do or may find difficult to do but the end result of that is never fear but freedom. Gods aim is always to set us free. However, bringing fear is never something that the voice of God brings. Our God has and is perfect love and perfect love casts out all fear. The voice of God will therefore always promote freedom over living in fear.[24]

God is never in a rush

When God speaks to us He never encourages us to rush things. Our God takes His time. He is certainly a quality over quantity God. Making you whole and making you free is the only priority of God's, how quickly He does it is not really His concern, we are usually the ones in a rush. For example, God gives us a vision for our life and if you're anything like me you get pretty excited and aim to rush and get it done. But I once read on twitter that God gives us our dreams and visions a few sizes too big so that we can grow into them and I believe this so very much. God can and does give us big dreams but it is our job to sit at the feet of Christ to be pruned, worked on and transformed in order for us to be able to fit well into the outfit he has prepared for us.

---

[24] "perfect love casteth out fear" 1 John 1:18 KJV

If we rush we can end up making a beautiful outfit look shabby and cheap because it's falling off us and is simply visibly too big. The voice of God therefore, will always encourage patience, because our God is never in a rush. I'm reminded of Lazarus' death and Mary's words to Jesus in the book of John. Mary stated to Jesus that had he have come sooner her brother would not have died. Mary failed to realise that Jesus came at the exact right time and what we consider late is so very much on time to God. He is a timeless God infact. He lives outside of time and simply created time. He is therefore never in a rush as He is timeless.

God is beautiful

Our God is a beautiful God. He therefore encourages all of His children that are made in His image that they too are oh so very beautiful. Any voice bringing you low self-esteem, telling you that you are not pretty enough, not smart enough, not kind enough or not whatever enough is the voice of the enemy feeding you lies. Rebuke that voice. The voice of God brings confidence in Him and the way He has created you, He fills you with the truth that you are fearfully and so wonderfully made. This reminds me of a song by an artist named Leah Smith which goes like this....

I've had those days where I wanted to be someone
else
Not good enough just being me
And I've had those times when I've looked into the
mirror
Not happy at all at what I'd see

'Cause I don't feel special
And I don't feel beautiful
And I don't feel smart enough, strong enough, good
enough - feel like nothing at all
But in times like these I come back to the truth that I
have found

I am beautifully and wonderfully made
I am beautifully and wonderfully made[25]

God calms you in the storm

The voice of God will always speak to you in the midst of the storm and calm you whilst the storm is taking place. Notice that is not to say storms will not come your way, but the voice of God will be your comforter in these times. He will not encourage you to lose your cool, go crazy, shout at somebody, get in a rage or act out in your flesh, the voice of God will be the still and quiet voice that

---

[25]http://www.lyrics.com/artists/lyricid/T%2017924429

you must listen out for in the midst of the storm telling you "it'll be more than ok".

God exposes

Our God is not a secrecy kind of God. He loves to expose things that are hidden in order to help heal us. God doesn't expose us to bring shame or humiliation. If there is a particular area of your life that God wants to bring to the light it is in order for Him to break the power of darkness over it. It is in order for Him to break the stronghold that the devil has over you and this secret or hidden way of living. He exposes to heal not to destroy. The devil would rather have us keep secrets that eat away at us and most times than none we would rather go the devils way and keep things a secret in order to avoid the pain of exposure. But I'd like to encourage you by saying this, bringing things to the light may hurt at first, but they set you free in the long run, and the God who led you to reveal and expose will not leave nor forsake you in seeing the whole thing through. Whether it is a friend you need to speak to, a confession you need to make, a spouse you need to expose something to, whatever it may be, go with the leading of the Holy Ghost and expose and bring the truth to light. God will honour your honesty and He will make the end result good even if it initially looks ugly. Remember the voice of the Lord encourages exposure for the purpose of healing and setting free, never to bring shame and bondage-keeping the lie will do that.

God promotes humility-joseph and his brothers.

The voice of God will always be the aid keeping you humble for God resists the proud, and gives grace to the humble.[26] I'd like to look at the story of Joseph for a little while. Joseph was shown a vision where He was the ruler of all of His brothers and He immediately came out and shared this with His brothers in a manner which I simply think could have been done differently. I believe the events that led to Joseph's imprisonment although a set up by God also acted as a humbling experience for Joseph. Keeping us humble and prideless is something that God so very much delights in. In the book of 1 Timothy verse 6 we read that as much as we bring nothing into this world surely we shall take nothing out of it.[27] This is very important to note. Nothing we acquire or gain in this world can ever match up to the love of God that is found in Christ Jesus.

---

[26] James 4:2 KJV

[27] 1 Timothy 6 KJV

God is funny!

I love this one! Our God is a funny God. He delights in joy, peace and fellowship. I believe one of the most pleasing things to God is when we don't take ourselves too seriously. When we come to God with a child like faith I guarantee you, you will laugh like never before at the smallest and silliest things. The voice of God will simply crack you up. Today, try not to take yourself too seriously, find the joy in the little things in life and laugh with God! He has many funny things lined up for you both to embark on.

God is LOVE

God is love and He can only speak loving things. God so loved us that He gave His only begotten son for us and to us. This same love is the love Jesus encourages us to have when He states in the book of John 13:34[28] that we love each other as He has loved us. Well how did Jesus love us? John 15: 13 tells us just this when we read that greater love hath no man but to lay down his life for his friends.[29] Would you lay down your life for a friend? Well

---

[28] Bible KJV

[29] Bible KJV

thank God that Jesus was the perfect sacrifice so we don't all need to go around laying down our lives for our friends (not that many of us would if we're honest). But my point is that the voice of God will encourage us to love one another with a pure heart. That is a heart with no motive but simply loving one another because we want to love and be good to one another. Loving our neighbours is something which the voice of God highly promotes.

> *If the voice you are hearing is teaching you how to be merciful, forgiving, fair, protecting, strong, fearless, patient, beautiful, calm, honest, humble, to laugh and to be full of love, Then yes...That is our God you are speaking with. Because slowly but surely His voice through the power of the Holy Ghost is conforming you to the image of Jesus Christ our Saviour as the scripture promises[30].*

---

[30] Romans 8:29 KJV

The Delivery Room

CHAPTER 8

UNHEALTHY TIES

What are unhealthy ties and how do we create them?

Unhealthy ties happen when we connect ourselves to any person that we had no business connecting ourselves to. You see we are spirit first; we simply live in a body. Those that we exchange with daily are also spirits first. Therefore when we become acquainted with people our spirits literally connect and there is a transfer. This is true with friendship; spouse, family and even those we work with. It is so important therefore, to keep in mind that when we associate ourselves with people we cannot see this as a casual thing that has no bearing on our lives; we must be very wise and take a long and deep think about the people that we allow to have an influence on our spirit man. Now I've known situations where people will be friends with someone that they don't particularly like, they cannot stand the person's flaws and their inner man. However, they continue to go to parties with this person and stay in extreme close communication with them thinking that they are able to control the influence that this individual is having on them. But no. You see our spirit man does not ask for our permission before he decides to make a transfer with the spirit man of another, this is literally done almost by osmosis. It is inevitable that what is in those that you surround yourself with will contaminate you; if not soon it sure will later.

You see this is why it is key that we watch the company that we keep. Our spirit man can become so emotionally attached to someone of the opposite sex that we begin to grow an unhealthy tie to this person. We cannot see our lives without them, we would do anything for them, we alter our character traits and do things that we never imagined we could ever do to please them or to get their attention. We watch how we dress, the words we choose to speak and spend countless hours with them. When this relationship breaks down we feel we cannot get over them, we cannot move on, we cannot ever see a life without them. Physiologists call this particular kind of scenario "strong emotional attachment". We it call love. *We* are wrong!

We are wrong for a number of reasons. I find it strange and honestly rather disrespectful to God that we call such a mess love. I find it even stranger that many people make statements such as "love is not easy, love is painful, with love comes pain" and so on. It is almost as though the whole world is trying to figure out what this love thing is. I'm sure we have all watched a movie where a 16 year old falls for her first boyfriend and begins to wonder "oh em gee what is this feeling?" She explains her symptoms to her mother and friends and she is diagnosed with "love". Her symptoms include "I can't stop thinking about him, he makes me feel special, he cares for me, our relationship has had its fair share of problems but we're really getting there" etc. She goes on to tell her boyfriend she loves him and he replies with the same 3 words and sure enough they are in "love". I am sure we have all been this 16 year old girl!

But you see recently God has been showing me that love is not some big mystery that we need to "work out" when we are feeling it. God has already told us what love is! There is already a ready made checklist that you can weigh your feelings up against to see if you are truly in love. This checklist is found in 1 Corinthians 13:4-8.

*Love is patient
*Love is kind
*It does not envy
*It does not boast
*It is not proud
*It does not dishonour others

*It is not self-seeking
*It is not easily angered
*It keeps no record of wrongs
*Love does not delight in evil but rejoices in the truth
*It always protects
*Always trusts
*Always hopes
*Always perseveres
*Love never fails

So now that we have the checklist lets go through it.

Love is patient.

Is the relationship that you are in one that promotes patience? Are you or your partner always seeking sexual moments with one another even though you are both aware that sex outside of the protection and gift of marriage is a sin? If yes then stop and ask yourself, is this love? Because God said, not me, but God Himself has told us that love is patient.

Love is also kind.

Are you and your partner kind to another without any hidden motives? Does he speak good and kind words to you and about you or does he put you down whether directly or indirectly?

Love does not envy.

Are you in a relationship that is fuelled with jealousy?

Love does not boast.

Are you using your relationship to boast against others? Is your self-worth in the fact that you are in a relationship?

Love is not proud.

Are you allowing yourself to remain with a prideful individual or do you have a lot of pride in you that you are bringing to the table?

Love does not dishonour others.

Are you being honoured as a woman? Are you respected? Is your body being respected? Are you respecting his? I.e. keeping your hands off one another until the day of marriage? Do you speak good of your partner whether he is around or not? Or do you bash him when you and your girlfriends get together?

Love is not self-seeking.

Are you both in the relationship for what you can get? Is he here for sex? Are you here for value and a sense of self-worth? Are you here because it's nice to have a boyfriend?

Love is not easily angered.

Is your relationship fuelled with anger and hurtful words and or actions?

Love keeps no record of wrongs.

Is your past constantly being dragged up? Are you dragging up his?

Love does not delight in evil but rejoices with the truth.

Is there honesty and truth in your relationship?

Love always protects.

Do you feel safe in your relationship? Does your heart feel safe? Or do you feel on edge and uneasy?

Do you feel like you will get hurt sooner or later? Is your heart in pain already?

Love always trusts.

Is your relationship fuelled with suspicion? Do you check up on him? Does he check up on you?

Love always hopes.

Do you have hope for your relationship? Do you truly believe that God's hand is in this and He is working? Or do you believe God wants you to leave?

Loves always perserveres.

Do you feel like you want to give up? Can you see yourself in this relationship for another 50 years? Can you continue to feel like this?

Love never fails.

Do you believe that your relationship can stand the test of time? No matter what comes your way will he always be there for you? Will he always stand by you?

Long list right?

Well the length of that list and the numerous questions to be asked and pondered over shows how seriously we are to take this person called love. I say person because God is love! He is the list we have just walked our way through. We cannot go around using the word love so loosely when in actual fact what many of us have and are holding unto is nothing but an unhealthy strong emotional attachment to another human being. If love is patient and kind and yet we have a man constantly trying his best to sleep with us or exercises no self-control in making sure that he does not attempt to tempt us, then he does not love us! He too, may simply be attached to us like we are attached to him. What a dirty cycle! This shows that more times than none what the world perceives to be two people in love are in fact just two people attached. It's the breaking off of this attachment that causes so many of us what is known as heartbreak. We then give love the blame when love was nowhere to be found in the unhealthy cycle that we created. Love does not bring sadness and love is not in the business of bringing two people together and then cruelly tearing them apart, causing them both such internal pain. God is love. To do that would make Him a wicked God and wicked He is not. He is good, He is true and He most certainly is not a liar. He told us that love perserveres, that means to say that love keeps on going, it never stops! Well we have so many marriages and relationships failing and breaking down every day. People have missed the essence of love. Because love carries on, love always hopes!

If after going through the list you are beginning to wonder if what you felt or are feeling is strong emotional attachment to another human being then please read on with me. If you have read through the list and are grinning from ear to ear because you have been blessed with a relationship that is truly love and not a negative attachment then we all praise God for you and pray that God continues to pour His love into your relationship. Read on with me also, it's always nice to reflect? Because remember, we can be negatively attached to anyone or anything, not just a member of the opposite sex.

How do I know if I am negatively attached to someone else?

I almost want to write here "you just know". Because the truth is, if you even have to ask yourself that question the chances are that you know exactly how, who and why. You just need to admit it to yourself! But of course if you're shy I'll happily lend you a helping hand.

You can know if you are negatively attached to someone when you cannot see your life aside from this person. Now I'm not speaking of a couple in love who enjoy being in love with another, I'm speaking of a crippling struggle to hold unto this person at all cost and yet they are not holding unto you in the same way. You cannot or are scared of the thought of a future aside from them. You have lost a sense of your own identity and you can no longer stand alone. You rely on them in an unhealthy way to boost your happiness, your self-esteem and yourself worth. What a shame. A queen, child of the most high God, beauty personified, cherished, pre-destined, known before you were even in your mother's womb, weaved together by the hands of an invisible God, more precious than the finest rubies, guarded by angels, power in your tongue and authority in your words and yet begging for attention as though a fatherless pauper. Let...him...go! And trust in the one who was, is and surely is to come. He will never leave you lonely. He will wipe every tear away from your eyes and will bring you out on the other side. It won't be easy, the pain may even seem unbearable, but let go anyway! Your heavenly Father is waiting to catch you...

Deuteronomy 31:6 NIV "Be strong and courageous, do not be afraid or terrified because of them, for the

Lord your God goes with you, he will never leave you nor forsake you...."

Extra teaching...

Now, unhealthy ties and attachments can come in many different forms. Of course some us may be in deeper than others and feel that every single point above relates to us, in that case that's ok as long as we admit it to ourselves and accept that help is needed. I can hear some of you thinking "well what if I'm married to or getting married to someone and I rely on them?" Well that's ok. Your husband is your blessing from God, rely on him all you want so much as is pleasing in God's eyes. However, it is still true that even your husband or fiancé can become someone that you grow an unhealthy attachment to if you are not careful. What do I mean? Well if you are a wife constantly checking through his phone for messages from other women (unhealthy), if you call his work place to make sure he's really where he says he is (unhealthy), if you control what he wears and who he is able to speak to and not speak to (unhealthy once again). No matter who it is we cannot go around life developing unhealthy attachments to other people or even things. Some of us develop unhealthy attachments to hair weave, makeup, our dogs or even the hope of designer items. We are so crazy sometimes!

Why is it bad for me that I am negatively attached?

Well aside from the simple reason that if the person that you are attached to is not attached to *you*, they will probably begin to find you to be the most irritating and annoying person on the planet, you are also just causing yourself so much strife and stress! Unhealthy attachments can never bring peace and joy, they bring worry and confusion and a bucket load of arguments. They also mean that you cannot ever birth the true you because your mind is overly preoccupied with this thing or person that is forever at the centre of your thoughts. You cannot live out your dreams fully and you cannot ever find true peace and joy. If in the context of a relationship, unhealthy ties or attachments will make you to believe that your life is not worth very much after the relationship is over. But that is a lie! Unhealthy attachments are often agents of lies. They will tell you things like "I can't move on, I can't get over him, I need him for my life to have any meaning". But this is not true. Your destiny is not tied to another person. Your destiny was given unto you even before you were even created as God says He knew you even before you were in your mother's womb (Jeremiah 1:5). So before you met "John" or "Simon" you had a purpose and your life had meaning. After "John" or "Simon" leave, you still have a purpose and your life will always have meaning! Your joy, peace, purpose, identity and self-worth should never be tied to another human being. All of these things lie in God and are found in God alone.

How do I break unhealthy attachments?

You know it's actually pretty simple and so I won't complicate it. Unhealthy attachments or ties develop as a result of habit. So begin to break the habits that led you to this point. Firstly if you are still in this relationship, break it off. If you are still calling him daily or he is calling you, stop! Change your number if you must. If you stalk him on Facebook - delete him! Take all of the necessary steps that are possible to ensure that you are free from this habit of self-destruction. Do you know that it's possible to even develop an unhealthy attachment to someone you have never met? You can be so taken in with someone, maybe a celebrity or so that you can literally become obsessed by all they do. We must simply take a look at the things we do that may be perceived as unhealthy and just stop doing them.

But of course the road can get difficult. It can get difficult because we can begin to miss all that we have ever known and our pattern of behaviour that we have become accustomed to. We may miss the person too, and missing someone is ok. However, it's important to keep in mind that we are doing this for our own good, we are letting go for our own good! And one day if we trust Him and look to Him, God will bring us the gift of love and gone will be the days of relationships fuelled with unhealthy ties or attachments and we can welcome relationships filled with love, peace and joy.

(For tips on how to abstain from returning to unhealthy ties, please take a look back to chapter 6 and the discussion surrounding a refusal to let go of the past).

The Delivery Room

CHAPTER 9

DRY YOUR EYES

Ever felt like you just can't stop crying? No matter how hard you try you just can't seem to pull yourself together. You're not even sure why you are crying or the reasons for your heartache, maybe there are too many things going on that you just don't know which issue triggered the tears today, or maybe nothing particularly bad is going on, which makes the cause of these tears all the more unexplainable and that in itself is enough to make you cry some more.

I have an answer for you… *Trust in the Lord with all of your heart and lean not on your own understanding.* (Proverbs 3:5-6 NIV)

The only times we feel restless and completely overwhelmed is when we are not resting in the present time that we are in. When we are allowing our past to creep in, our future to scare us and our immediate tomorrow to keep us anxious we cannot possibly experience the peace of God. As a young woman I understand what it can be like living in the 21st century and dealing with a million and one things that can attempt to bring us to tears and leave us drowning in a state of depression each and every day. From feeling insecure about the way we look, constant diets, running the rat race of gaining a boyfriend or the need to get married and have a first baby by 30 it can all be so overwhelming. But here's a question for you... who told you these things?

Who told you that you are not beautiful?

The world did, the media did, the boys at your school did when they chose to run after the other girls at school and not you. Your "best friends" did when they made gentle and not so under cover digs at you as you all got ready for a night out. For some of you it's worse because maybe a family member did, maybe even your mum did, maybe everyone in your family never stops letting you know that you are the "ugly" one. But here's the thing, no matter who told you this, they are a liar! And we don't listen to liars. We listen to God.

Your heavenly Father who decided that the world wouldn't be complete without you in it, who decided that He would place a value on you that was far above rubies, who decided that He would take you from a foetus and guide you so gently and safely until this day, that is the person that you listen to. He tells you that you are wonderfully and fearfully made and that each hair on your head is counted, He knows your going in and your coming out and knows when you sit and when you stand, He loves you beyond measure and He would never lie to you and He says you are perfect.

Who told you that you are not complete until you have a boyfriend?

Your insecurities did, your low self-esteem did, your jealousy of your friends in their own relationships did, your lack of patience in waiting on God's perfect timing did, thinking and believing that you need to be in the same point of life as other people did, not liking your own company did, playing the comparison game did, but God did not. All of these other voices are liars. Refuse to be lied to. God tells you that you are made complete in Him. You do not need a boyfriend to know that you are somebody or that you are special, you are already special in the sight of God.

Who told you that you must be married by 30 and have your first child?

The media did, watching celebrities and their desire of this did, the world did and your fears of never being wanted by a man did. I heard a story the other day of a woman who had known God since the age of 21 and was waiting on His perfect timing for her to be married. God's perfect timing for her came at the age of 53. Wow! Imagine if this was you? Could you wait so patiently for God's perfect timing?

Ladies we cannot set a time bar and expect God to meet the deadline. God will not give you something before its due time and will not cause you to hurt yourself by granting you an untimely gift.

So...if any of the above were reasons for your tears then you must know this, you are not in control of your life and learning to accept this fact will bring you so much peace. If you want control over the steering wheel of your life you sure can take back control but here is the problem, you will lead yourself blindly down a destructive path and will end up playing a guessing game with your own heart. But when God is in control, He knows the end from the beginning and will never lead you astray or cause you to stumble. With God you will never walk in the dark for He is the light of this world and the light in your everyday life. Believe that He cares for you and that is the only reason why He is taking His time to birth the awesome things that lie within you.

God is watching over you

Every tear that you cry is seen by the Most High. It breaks His heart to see you cry. Your heavenly Father loves you beyond what words could describe; when you bruise He bruises also. Trust Him that He would never let you down. If you have tried everything else then surely He is the last hope that you can cling unto anyway? If you give up on God sis what do you actually have left? You know I used to feel hopeless at one time in my life, but then I realised that God was my hope and that if I had Him I had everything that I could ever need. No, things didn't get better instantly but my heart strengthened as the days went by and slowly but surely joy and peace filled my heart.

I made a decision not to allow fear and sadness to rule my heart but to allow the Most High who is my hiding place to be my anchor, the one I could hold unto in good times and bad. One of the things that I struggled with was simply being myself, but I allowed Him to tell me that I was beautiful, I allowed Him to tell me how to dress and not to feel like I had to wear what everyone else was wearing. Being 5"10 I remember wanting to shop for 6 inch heels like every other female but feeling uncomfortable with the idea of towering over what seemed like the whole world, and you know what God told me… "you don't have to do or wear anything you don't want to, you are beautiful to me", what a freedom that brought me. The devil is a liar and would have had me always feeling insecure about something so trivial, but God had freedom set up for me. Praise God!

I realised that whenever any sort of lie came into my mind (and the enemy lies to us all just about every single day about almost every single thing) I had to go directly to my God (my Abba and my source) and ask Him about His opinion on that matter. I can trust my Father to tell me the truth, I cannot and will not trust any other voice. Any other voice other than the voice of the Holy Ghost, the person of the Holy Spirit, is the voice of a lie.

You see sis it's believing these lies that are causing you to cry, whatever it is that the enemy is allowing you to think or believe that is what is bringing you sadness and a state of depression. Why not go to your heavenly Father and ask His opinion on the matter….I promise you He will always tell you the truth. Take a look back at chapter 7 for some guidance on how to hear the Lord's voice and begin to dry your eyes.

Rooting for you always….x

CHAPTER 10

LIVING FOR MORE THAN ME!

Living for you only? Well another way to ensure we give birth to the true us is to keep in mind that we are living for more than us. Living for ourselves alone will cause us misery and pain and will bring no fulfillment to our lives. We will simply never be satisfied, never be content, never be useful and will never experience the true power of God which is the dynamic power of love. It is undeniable the level of joy and reward that comes from a life that is truly lived out for others and lived out for God and for His divine purpose. Jesus demonstrated this when He went beyond Himself and lay His life down for us on the cross. He exemplified love in its purest and most uncontaminated form when He lived a selfless life and performed such a selfless act. He lived for His father whose will it was for Him to give Himself up as a sacrifice, and He lived for us that we may be able to come into relationship with the Father and that our sins would not mean a life of condemnation in Hell. His selfless act brought Him a reward of a seat on the right hand of the Father. It is important therefore that when we make decisions we make them keeping in mind the purpose of living for God and living for others. This means that sometimes the things that we want to do we cannot do because we keep in consideration how it may affect others and the impact it would have on God's purpose for our lives. For example, I could decide today that I want to go wild and have a super rebellious day and do things that are very not Christ like. Even if I desperately wanted to do this it is important for me to keep in mind that others that are looking to me may be affected by this and the plan of God for my life may be affected by this. Living for God and others therefore also allows me to keep on the straight path.

Now I think this is extremely important for the single ladies. When the time comes to pick a spouse why not be unselfish and not think about just what you want but keep in mind also that you are living for more than yourself. Your life and your decisions whether you like it or not directly or indirectly affect the lives of others. So, when choosing a spouse why not keep these things in mind; is this a man that I would want my children to have as a father? Would he make a good father? Would he do anything for us? Would he provide for us? Would my children be proud to have this man as their father?! You see taking the focus off you allows you to also see the situation a lot clearer as you are not simply clouded by your emotions. I started to write a blog a little while ago and wrote an insert which I think could help you understand this point even better. I called this insert "Letters to my daughters daughter".

Letters to my daughter's daughter (04-11-2011)

I have no idea where to start, what to write or where this is going. I just feel to write? I don't know your name, what you look like or how you sound, but I do know that you are my daughter's daughter and so you are a part of me. You are my responsibility. You are a product of my thoughts, decisions and actions.

Lately God has been speaking to me about preparing a legacy for my children's children. The more He spoke to me about it, though not in so many words but more so in gut feeling and remembrance, the more I began to truly wish to leave you with a lasting legacy. In all honestly I initially felt a fool for thinking about this, I'm only 22? Why am I thinking about my children's children at the age of 22? I'm young, carefree and should be enjoying the prime of life right? However the one word which kept coming back to me was Responsibility. How you turn out, the sort of woman you become, the morals and values that you hold, those are all my responsibility, and 22 yes I may be, but this is one 22 year old that is ready to step up to my responsibility.

I want you to be proud of your mother, my daughter. I want you to be thankful of the way I raised her and the morals that I instilled in her that she has passed down to you. I want you to be proud of the man she chose to make your father because of the values I taught her on how a man should treat a lady and how a lady should serve a man. I want you to cherish the faith and spirituality that you look forward to sharing with your children because grandma dedicated her life to God and loved serving Him and was such close friends with Him. I deeply desire for you to one day have a conversation with God about me and for Him to tell you about mine and His relationship and for you both to laugh and enjoy the memories that He and I once shared. But before all of this is possible I know I must set the ground running now.....

Now, when I make decisions I make them with you in mind. I think about the man that I will marry and do not think selfishly on who I want because I want them, but I want to be with a man who will make a wonderful and committed father to your mother. A man, who will teach her by example of how a man is to treat a lady, take care of a lady, provide for and cherish a lady. A man who you will be proud to call your grandfather. I do not ever wish for you to think of your grandfather and be ashamed of the man that I chose to be with and wish that I had chosen differently. I hate the thought of you sitting with your girlfriends whilst you all discuss marriage and you uttering the words "I don't want my marriage to be like all the women in my family"....instead I want you to sit at mine and your grandfathers 60th wedding anniversary and look on with pride and admiration and whisper to God above.... "I want that".

I want you to come from a family line of good women, not necessarily great women in terms of deeds or actions, but good women with good hearts who put their God, husbands and children before all things.

Now I may not know you yet but im sure you'll be beautiful (you're a part of me of course you will be haha). But I want to teach you how to appreciate your outer beauty but to understand that there is a far more precious type of beauty which radiates from the inside out. I want you to learn all about integrity, sisterhood, honesty, decency, self worth and self love. I want you to have a wonderful life filled with love, peace, joy and fulfilment. I want you to be a great wife to your husband (a great support system, his backbone and his friend), a great mother to your children (their cook, their cleaner, their friend, their voice of reason, their number 1 go to person), I want you to be a lover of God (His child, His friend, His reliable daughter). But I know before you can be all of these things...I must firstly become all of these things....

I am trying my best to become the woman that will be able to pass all of these things down to you. You will be my legacy, and I want you to reflect the woman that I was. I am watching my actions, my words and my thoughts. I am keeping you in mind when I make decisions on who to date, where to go, what to say, what friends I should keep, what church I should attend, what prayers I should pray. I am no longer living a selfish life. I am stepping up to the plate and becoming a woman who is thinking about her children's children. It's no longer about me but it's about us. It's about what our family will stand for, what we will be known for and the legacy that we will leave. It's certainly not easy because to be quite honest most of the time I just want to do what others are doing, and I can, but I won't. I won't because I've come to understand that the actions that I make today will affect you tomorrow. If I decide to join a cult you will always have a cultish root in your family line. If I decide to drink without care you will have an alcoholic trait in your family line. If I decide to sleep around you will always have a harlot spirit in your family line. If I decide to backbite and bitch you will also have the seed of a lack of integrity. If I decide to be lazy you will always have an idol mindset. If I decide to marry a man because I want him and fail to think about how he would be as a father and as a man you will always come from a fatherless generation. If I decide to be a disobedient wife you will never understand what it takes to keep a marriage together and the patience and endurance that a woman must have in order to remain a good woman able to keep a good home. I do not wish to pass these things down to you; I wish to pass down to you all good things. These will be my legacy to you.

Lots of love; your mother's mother.

Hi there reader!

I hope that by reading the note above to my daughter's daughter you have been inspired to no longer live with the illusion that you live for yourself alone. In proverbs 13:22 it says that "A good man leaves an inheritance for his children's children, but a sinner's wealth is stored up for the righteous". Although the scripture appears to be talking about financial wealth I believe leaving an inheritance doesn't always have to be about monetary affairs or land etc, it definitely can and does refer to us leaving behind the things that money can't buy.

It's a huge responsibility that we have but we can fulfil this so easily. Simply just by working on our own character and our own flaws and working towards perfecting those daily. No one is without their struggles and no one is without blemish, but understanding that we cannot live selfishly with the ideology of believing that no one else is affected by our actions is key. I hope that by reading this you are able to begin your journey to leaving a good and fruitful legacy for your children's children. Allow your seed and their seed to be proud of the woman they came from.

K.Ashanike xx-xx

I love love love that blog! It inspires me daily to want to make life decisions with others in mind. Now, it's also important to live life with God's purpose in mind, which leads me unto my next point which is eradicating the mentality of living with a self centredmindset.

Putting it simply it's important to then come to a realisation: the realisation that it's not all about you. The plain truth is that we have become a self centered people, where everything simply revolves around us. We have become so consumed with seeking the things of God but never seeking God Himself. Yes we say "oh I'm seeking the Father" but in all truth and brutal honesty we have become a people who mostly only want to pray to God for blessings. When you have gone past the issues of rejection etc it's important to now know that you are no longer your own and it's not all about you, it never even was. It was merely the deluded belief of our "own" self importance that made us think it was all about us. Remember that the devil is a deceiver, for so long he has deceived us that God doesn't love us or can't love us but now he may deceive us into believing that God is merely there to bless us. Yes God is a rewarder of those that diligently seek Him and oh how He very much delights in blessing His children, but there is such a joy in simply coming to know God and His beautiful nature that to merely seek His hands is causing ourselves to miss out on something so much greater. There is a reward that will overwhelm us that God has in store for us that far surpasses anything we can ever even think of. Jesus stated in the book of John 14 that in His Father's house are many houses and that He goes to create a place for us. Can you imagine that! The God of heaven and earth loves us so much that He makes way for His son to create a special place for us ahead of our home coming. That alone should inspire us to live our lives for the sake of eternity and keep eternity in mind always. This would allow such goodness to flow into our lives because whenever we are tempted to live a life without laws, without wise decisions and for our own selfish wants, we are able to keep in mind that we live for more than ourselves, and our actions can and do affect others and the overall purpose of God for our lives, positively or negatively.

If you are someone that has already made a bad decision, made bad choices and headed down a bad road please understand that His love covers and His grace is greater than our mistakes, greater than our past, greater than our failures and so much greater than our fears. Come on back home and get back in alignment with Him... I can promise you He has been patiently waiting for you and welcomes you back with open arms!

The Delivery Room

CHAPTER 11

DON'T RUSH THE PROCESS

It's now also important to keep in mind that healing is a process. Although I have attempted to walk you through some pointers and some key issues please keep in mind that there is truly no quick fix. You simply have to go through. Now depending on you as a person healing can take anything from weeks to months to years. You can have two girls that experience a terrible breakup and whilst it takes one 3 months to get over the hurt and pain it may take another 3 years. That's ok! As long as you are not unnecessarily longing out the process but allowing God to walk you through a journey plan that is suitable for you. I wrote a second blog entry which I believe will allow you to understand why taking your time is key. I called this one "Birth before the due date".

Birth Before the Due Date

Conception

It all begins with a single sperm seed and a woman is conceived with something that isn't even the size of a peanut. But this "peanut" is to become a human being filled with emotions, a purpose, a dynamic personality. This "peanut" will one day become a father, an author, a speaker, a king, a prime minister, a business mogul. However, before this "peanut" can become all of these things and begin to impact the world around him he is to firstly endure a period of growth and learning. This period I call "Transformation".

Transformation

During this stage our "peanut" begins to grow and starts to look like a person. He begins to have hands, feet, the brain starts to function, the body truly becomes that of a real person. Following the transformation period our peanut which is now a fully matured looking baby will still spend time in its mother's belly to simply get accustomed to its surroundings and learn to use all of the things that he has now developed such as kicking his new feet, poking with his new fingers etc. Following the transformation period is the "Birth".

Birth

Once the time to push arrives there is no denying that it is time. As far as I'm aware no woman has ever given birth naturally without feeling any level of pain whatsoever. What was once a peanut now becomes a real life human being wanting to fight its way out.

I believe that this birthing process is the same way that God works with us. This peanut is an idea, a relationship, a promise, a future, a whatever it is that God has deposited into your heart. However, we must wait before this "thing" can become exactly what God has called it to be and not give birth to a cheap or tacky version of it.

Any woman's worst nightmare is going into labour months before her due date. She is aware that early labour is a sign of something being severely wrong. Any dream or promise birthed before God's time is an increased danger of giving birth to a dead baby, a disabled baby or baby that will struggle and be required to fight for life. All of this causing severe pain and heartache for the mother. We are all carriers of dreams, desires and promises of what Abba has given us, but we must ensure not to push too soon. We all have a tendency to run ahead and deliver something because He has given it to us NOW so we believe it is for NOW. However, God blesses a woman with a baby in January yet the baby is a gift for September. He plants the seed but we must wait for Him to nourish what He has planted in us before we begin to push.

Well When do I push?

A lot of people fear missing out on God's plan for them, or the one I hear often "missing out on what God is doing NOW!" Well God does not slumber nor sleep so rest assured He's always doing something. Clearly! God will never leave you behind if your heart is right before Him and your desires towards Him are pure. We must also be careful not to allow ourselves to be manipulated by others with talks of "missing out" or even allow ourselves to scare ourselves into thoughts of "missing out" that we begin to push before our due date causing ourselves to run ahead of God. I would so rather miss out completely because I was waiting on Him than to run ahead of God and not only miss out on what He was doing but miss HIM completely. And we so have it easy! When a woman's time has come to push she sure as heck knows it's time to push. No one has to tell her that...she'll know!

But aside of the "when to push" a lot of us also worry about; "well if I leave it, if I let go of the dream, the promise, the "whatever" it may be, and trust that God will birth it when its time how do I know God hasn't forgotten?". Or worse still, "if I don't DO anything then nothing will happen so I'll have nothing to birth anyway." Not true.

Learning to mind your own business

During her pregnancy a woman cannot see what is going on inside her belly, she couldn't see when the sperm and the egg met and she sure can't see when the eyes are growing, the fingers are growing or the brain is forming. It's the one time when we are totally out of control of what is happening with our own bodies. But she always trusts that something is happening. Why? Because she is growing!...the growth happening in her is a testimony to the fact that what she has been blessed with is being taken care of and is growing bigger and bigger each day. All she needs to do to focus on giving birth to a healthy baby is to eat right and take care of herself! If she fails to take care of herself she puts her baby in danger. You need not focus on the "thing" that you carry! Focus on you and your personal relationship with Him and the thing that you carry will automatically be taken care of. When you make a close and intimate relationship with God your business He makes your business His business.

We all spend so much time worrying about when things will happen. When will that promise come to pass and when will this "thing" happen that we almost force and encourage ourselves into an early labour. We push and continue to push something that is not yet ready to be birthed....when we push some more we then go to pray some more or fast some more or pray some more again and then cry some more and some more again and say "God but you promised me".....We fail to see that God isn't denying that He promised it...He's simply saying "not now". Sometimes we are ok with hearing the not now and wait, but the danger comes with the times when we continue to push and hold a determination to give birth to it anyway. It's no surprise we end up in scarring relationships, with failed businesses, struggling friendships and awful mindsets, and the like. Anything birthed before God's time will always cause pain, distress, strive, confusion and heartache. Instead of worrying about why and how long we should wait for, lets enjoy the pregnancy stage of our lives and worry more about the great danger that comes with going into an early labour. And remember your due date is never the same as anyone else's, your friends due date could be years before yours, years after yours or a world apart from yours. Run your own race....and learn to wait.

"Those that wait upon on the Lord shall renew their strength; they shall mount up with wings as eagles; they shall run, and not be weary, and they shall walk, and not faint"....Isaiah 40:31

Hey there Sis, I love that blog also! Although it doesn't directly speak on healing I think we can take some pointers from it to help us on our journey of delivery. For example, when it speaks on minding your own business when it comes to the pregnancy stage this is very important for us also when it comes to a healing process. It's important to understand that God is taking you through a difficult time, accept that it's a difficult time but rejoice that God is with you during it and is walking you through it and be thankful that you are not alone. Minding your own business is key because it allows you to focus not on "when are we going to get there" but to simply listen to the instructions that God is giving to you every step of the way. For example, delivering the true us is the whole purpose of this book, i.e creating wholeness and being full of joy in Christ, however, we don't focus on that from the get go, we have gone step by step and started with obedience, then willingness, then rejection, then loneliness and so on. It's important to give your undivided attention to each stage and not worry so much about the end, just trust Him to lead you and you simply take it healing by healing until you reach total restoration. Sooner or later you will reach your destination of fullness and joy in Christ Jesus and as the blog spoke, the whole world will see the birthing of the goodness that Christ has done in you.

CHAPTER 12

A NEW WAY OF LIVING

And here is my most favourite part! Total restoration and redemption. Tears are literally filling my eyes as I write this chapter because I know what it is like to reach this place sis and I am so excited for you and pray with all of my heart that you too reach this place.

Wow. How awesome is God. No matter what you go through in this life, on the other side of your obedience lies a crown of beauty for ashes and He will give you the oil of gladness for mourning, there will be no more crying and everything will be made brand new. I sit writing this chapter a few days into making the decision to take my own advice and trust God and self publish this book. We are now in 2013 and I wrote what used to be the very first chapter of this book in 2009. God is so faithful. He has literally guided me and has been my navigating system and my strength to carry on. I look back at the girl I was at 19 when I started this book and was given the title "The Delivery Room" and look now, 5 years on, at the woman that has been delivered in *me* whilst I wrote encouraging others to deliver *themselves*. God leaves me speechless. At the age of

19 I couldn't even dream the stuff that God has done, He has blessed me with a beautiful ministry in Pure Hearts, He has opened doors for me on radio, He has even healed my fear of flying to allow me to travel to India to be apart of an amazing conference and pray for other people, He has led young women to me and trusted me with their hearts and allowed me to encourage other people and pray for them, He has led me through university, I have seen my family saved, I have seen God save people that I at one time would have bet could have never been saved, He has humbled me, changed me, set me free, changed my mind set and has shown me that everything that I thought I was, I wasn't, and everything that I thought I couldn't be, I am. I pray the same for you sis and I know that if God could fill me with peace and joy He sure can and will for you too.

> *A new way of living has filled my heart. His Kingdom has come and has truly come in this earthly vessel that is I.*

So is everyday perfect? No sis, every day is not perfect, but He is showing me that I am perfect in Him everyday.

How can I have a new way of living I hear you say? Well you're already on the road to allowing His

Kingdom to come in your life. By shifting aside and dealing with all of the things that you have dealt with in the previous chapters you are already automatically making room for this new way of life to manifest itself.

Now here are some pointers, some things that you can do to ensure this new life of His Kingdom reigns in your life.

Don't be scared of people

I had to learn that what other people thought about me wasn't important. In a world where many young women were making YouTube videos about makeup and hair I was making YouTube videos about waiting on the One. When other people were out I was indoors working on Pure Hearts, when other people could wear what they wanted I was very careful about what I wore and what I said knowing full well that God intended on using me one day and I couldn't and wouldn't make a spectacle of Him or have other young women think it was ok to wear or dress in a certain way. I was being careful because I knew I was now to live in a new way and had been set free for a purpose. I no longer was shy to tell people that I was waiting on God to release me into ministry in His own time when people would ask why I wasn't going to law school or what were my plans for the next five years, I simply (by the power of God in me giving me boldness) didn't really care anymore what people thought. I wasn't scared of the reaction of others and knew that God had called me for a bigger purpose.

Whilst I continue to wait on the manifestation of that purpose I exercise my faith daily in Him knowing that whilst I wait He will strengthen my heart (Psalm 27:14).

It's funny because once I wasn't shy about being honest about who I was, and didn't care that half my followers on instagram were not Christians, and I still went ahead and posted daily scriptures I started seeing girls come to me and were able to be open about the truth of what they were experiencing or when they wanted some guidance. I even had one of my Muslim colleagues send me a text thanking me for me for a video I had made that gave her clarity about a certain situation she was dealing with. My point is, when you choose to live in a new way and do so with courage and knowledge of exactly who you are in Christ then you indirectly give those around you the power to do so also.

<u>Do not be Afraid</u>

Don't be scared Sis about your future or what will happen to you. You know the other day I realised that I had a lot of anxiety and God said to me, "You are sacred that I'm going to let you down". So sad. I wonder how many of us feel like this. How many of us are scared that God will not come through for us like He promised. I am working on that I tell you. I know deep within my heart that He would never let me down, I guess the circumstances of life can make us scared that He will. I prayed hard that God take away that feeling of fear of disappointment and can only continue to pray that He clear my heart of all such anxiety. I know that we cannot be afraid of the things that God has called us to do and cannot be scared of our future. I can tell you that it is hard for me even now knowing what tomorrow holds. I truly don't have a plan, every plan that I have had God has wiped away (lol because I can only laugh at that) but I do know this, I may not know what tomorrow holds but I do know the one who holds my tomorrow.

So…if there are any last words that I can leave with you sis its this, well done for enduring the process of healing, well done for not giving up, do not be afraid of the healing process and all that God wants to heal in you, do not be afraid of people and what they might think of you when God begins to change you and do not be afraid of what tomorrow holds.

May our Abba father keep you and be with you always...your future is bright if you leave it in His hands...x

The Delivery Room

10937714R00093

Printed in Great Britain
by Amazon.co.uk, Ltd.,
Marston Gate.